The Ceiling Instinct

The Financial Self-Sabotage Pattern That Keeps Bringing You Back Down

Jordan Ellis

First edition, 2026

Published by Jordan Ellis

Contents

Foreword	1
Introduction	5
Chapter 1 — The Thermostat You Didn't Set	23
Chapter 2 — The Alarm Purchase	41
Chapter 3 — The Ask You Didn't Make	59
Chapter 4 — The Generous Leak	77
Chapter 5 — The Bet That Wasn't Like You	95
Chapter 6 — The Deal You Talked Yourself Out Of	113
Chapter 7 — The Discount You Keep Giving Yourself	131
Chapter 8 — The Raise That Didn't Last the Month	149
Chapter 9 — The Room You Made Yourself Smaller In	167
Before You Go	185
Notes & Further Reading	199
About This Book	209
Also in the Series	215

Foreword

I've spent a long time watching smart, capable people describe their own financial reversals as bad luck — a market that turned, a client who fell through, a "weird year." I've spent almost as long noticing how often those explanations don't survive contact with the calendar. Line the setbacks up against the wins that came just before them, and the pattern gets hard to unsee. This book started there, in the gap between what people were telling themselves and what their own dates were telling me.

I didn't set out to write about a ceiling. I set out to write about lifestyle creep — the slow, familiar drift everyone already has language for. But the closer I looked at how people actually described their own reversals, the more I kept running into something that wasn't drift at all. It was sudden. It arrived on a schedule you could set a clock to: within days of the raise, within weeks of the milestone, right after the number everyone had been working toward for years. Creep explains the slow leak. It doesn't explain the flinch.

That flinch is the reason this book exists. Not an abstract interest in self-sabotage — this specific, repeatable flinch, the same timing attached to it story after story. I don't think the people living through it are broken, or secretly afraid of money in some dramatic sense, and this book argues against that reading directly. I wrote it because the flinch is real, common, mechanical rather than moral, and almost nobody carrying it has a name for it. Most have spent years blaming themselves for a reflex installed before they had any say in the matter — and that misdiagnosis costs more than the money ever does. It costs them the belief that they're capable of holding what they build.

What earned this its own volume, rather than a paragraph inside a broader book, is how precisely the timing gives it away once you're looking for it. Line up someone's last four high points against what happened in the weeks after each one, and the coincidence stops looking like coincidence. Name the mechanism, and the shame attached to it starts to loosen — often before a single override in this book has even been tried.

That loosening is the point. Not the theory underneath it. The moment someone stops calling it bad luck.

— Jordan Ellis

Introduction

You hit a new high point, and something in you flinched.

Maybe it was a number on a screen — the first time your savings crossed a threshold you'd been circling for years. Maybe it was a deal closing, a raise landing, a business finally turning the corner you'd been pushing it toward for eighteen months. Whatever the shape of it, there was a moment — brief, almost too brief to notice — where the feeling wasn't triumph. It was something closer to vertigo. A held breath. A flicker of *this isn't right* underneath the part of you that was supposed to be celebrating. And then, within days or weeks, something happened that brought the number back down. Not a market crash. Not a layoff. Something you did. An unplanned purchase that made no sense against your stated goals. A bet you wouldn't have made a month earlier. A conversation you sabotaged, a deal you let slip, a raise you talked yourself out of asking for twice as hard as you'd been building toward it. You didn't plan any of it. You'd have denied, in the moment, that it was connected to the high point at all. But it was.

This book is about that flinch, and about the invisible number underneath it that the flinch is protecting.

Here is the master thesis, the one sentence this entire book exists to earn: *you have an internal number for what you believe you're allowed to have, and whenever your actual finances rise above it, some part of you will act — quietly, plausibly, and against your own stated interest — to bring them back down to where they feel correct.* Not because you're self-destructive. Not because you secretly don't want money. Because a number that exceeds what feels like *you* doesn't register as good news. It registers as an error. And errors, to the part of the mind responsible for keeping your sense of self stable, get corrected.

This is different from the more familiar story about money and self-sabotage, the one about lifestyle creep — the slow, gradual expansion of spending that eats a raise before you've had a chance to feel it, one subscription and one upgraded car and one nicer apartment at a time. Creep is real, and it's worth naming, and if you want the fullest account of it, that's a different book's territory. But creep is gradual. It's drift. It happens so slowly that by the time you notice, you can't point to the day it started. What this book is about is not drift. It's a reflex — sudden, specific, and triggered by a single identifiable event: the moment you cross a line you didn't know you'd drawn. Creep is water level rising so slowly you don't feel wet. The ceiling is a hand reaching up and pulling you back down the instant your head clears the surface. Both cost you money. Only one of them happens the moment you succeed.

You'll recognize the shape once you start looking for it, because it doesn't announce itself as sabotage — it announces itself as a series of individually reasonable decisions. A man gets the promotion he's wanted for three years, and within a month he's put a down payment on a boat he can't really afford and doesn't have time to use. A woman closes the biggest client contract of her freelance career and, four days later, loans a struggling sibling an amount of money that quietly erases the entire signing bonus. A couple pays off the last of their debt for the first time in a decade, feels the genuine relief of it for about two weeks, and then one of them — without discussing it, without really deciding it — starts making the kind of impulse purchases that will have new debt rebuilding within the year.

None of these people would tell you they're afraid of money. Each of them would give you a perfectly good reason for the purchase, the loan, the impulse buy — reasons true enough on their own terms. The boat really was a good deal. The sibling really did need help. The purchases really were things they'd wanted for a while. What none of them would tell you, because none of them consciously know it, is that the decision arrived within days of crossing a number, and that timing is not a coincidence. It's the mechanism working exactly as designed.

The mechanism has a name, and it isn't mysterious once you see it named. Psychologists who study the self have long documented something called self-verification — the deep, largely unconscious drive people have to keep the world confirming what they already believe about themselves, even when that belief is unflattering, even when disconfirming evidence would objectively be good news. If somewhere underneath your conscious self-talk you believe you're someone who has "this much" money and no more — a belief formed decades ago, often long before you had any real financial agency at all — then evidence that you now have more doesn't feel like relief. It feels like dissonance. A gap has opened up between the self you know yourself to be and the self the bank statement is now describing, and dissonance, uncorrected, is intolerable. Something has to close the gap. Usually, it's not a conscious decision to lose the money. It's a small, plausible, real-world action that has the effect of closing it — and closing it fast enough that the discomfort resolves before you've even had time to name what you were feeling.

This is not a book about willpower, and it's not a book that will tell you to simply "believe in abundance" harder, because that framing gets the mechanism backwards. The problem was never that you don't believe you deserve more. Plenty of people who self-sabotage at the ceiling would tell you, sincerely, that they want more, that they're working for more, that they'd love nothing more than to finally break through. The problem is that wanting and believing are two entirely different systems, and only one of them is running the show when the money actually arrives. You can want a higher number with your whole conscious mind and still carry, underneath it, an old and unexamined figure that some much younger version of you decided — correctly, given the evidence available at the time — was the ceiling. Fixing this isn't about wanting harder. It's about finding the old figure, seeing it clearly, and updating it the way you'd update any belief that was formed under conditions that no longer apply.

There's also a question worth asking before we go further: why does this happen specifically around a threshold, a felt line crossed, rather than just gradually, the way most psychological accounts of money behavior tend to describe it? The answer is that thresholds are how self-concept actually tracks the world. You don't experience your net worth as a smooth continuous line — nobody wakes up and consciously registers that their savings grew by forty-one dollars overnight. What you register, if you register anything at all, are the round numbers, the milestones, the moments a mental category flips from "not yet" to "now" — the first time savings cross five figures, the first time a paycheck starts with a different number of digits, the first time "what I have" and "what I always assumed people like me have" stop matching. Categories are binary in a way continuous quantities aren't. You are either inside the category "someone who has this much" or you're not, and the moment you cross into a category your self-concept never certified you for, the mismatch registers all at once, sharply, rather than gradually. That's why the reflex is event-triggered rather than gradual, and it's the single clearest thing separating this book's territory from lifestyle creep, which by contrast is a slow, uncategorized drift with no single moment of crossing at all.

Consider two people who would seem, on paper, to have nothing in common. The first is a software engineer in her early thirties who grew up genuinely poor — not "we didn't take vacations" poor, but the kind of poor where the electricity got shut off twice one winter and her mother cried over grocery receipts. She is, now, extremely good at her job, well compensated, and has been offered a role with a significant raise three separate times over four years. Each time, she has found a reason to decline — the timing wasn't right, she wasn't ready for the responsibility, she preferred her current team. Each reason was sincere. None of them, examined honestly, holds up against the fact that she is, by every external measure, exactly the person the new role was designed for. The second is a contractor in his fifties who grew up in a household that was comfortable, even a little affluent, but where his father — successful, admired, exhausting to be around — made money the entire currency of value in the house, so that being loved and being financially impressive became fused into a single, inseparable thing. This man has built and nearly lost three businesses. Each time, the business grew to roughly the size his father's had been at its peak — and then, at almost exactly that point, something happened. A partnership he trusted too quickly. A expansion he made against every piece of advice he was given. A refusal to raise prices that any objective observer would have called overdue. Two entirely different childhoods. Two entirely different flavors of self-sabotage. The same underlying mechanism: an old, internal number, installed long before either of them could evaluate it, quietly overriding every conscious financial decision they now make as adults.

That's the pattern this book exists to name, chapter by chapter, in its different disguises — because the ceiling doesn't wear one costume. Sometimes it looks like an impulsive purchase timed suspiciously close to a windfall. Sometimes it looks like sabotaging the negotiation itself, before the money even arrives — going quiet in the salary conversation you'd rehearsed for weeks, or underpricing the deal you know is worth more. Sometimes it looks like generosity, which is the hardest disguise to see through, because who's going to argue with helping a struggling relative or over-tipping a stranger? Sometimes it looks like risk — a bet placed, a trade made, a bad investment entered into with a carelessness that doesn't match how careful you are about everything else — that has the specific, almost surgical effect of returning your number to where it "should" be. Sometimes it doesn't touch the money at all; it touches the deal, the relationship, or the opportunity that would have produced the money, and sabotages that instead, so the number never has to rise past the line in the first place. Eight chapters, eight shapes. Different scenes, different triggers, different disguises. The same reflex underneath all of them.

There's a reasonable objection worth addressing directly, because if you don't resolve it now it will quietly undermine every chapter that follows: doesn't this sound a little too convenient? Any unplanned purchase, any stalled negotiation, any bad bet could, after all, be explained away as "the ceiling" if you're determined enough to see it everywhere. That objection is fair, and this book takes it seriously rather than waving it off, because a framework that explains everything actually explains nothing — it just becomes a new, more sophisticated story to hide behind. The way to hold this honestly is to treat the ceiling not as a diagnosis you apply to any single event, but as a hypothesis you test against a pattern across time. One purchase after one high point tells you almost nothing. The same purchase, in different clothing, showing up within weeks of your last four or five financial high points — the promotion, the payoff, the closed deal, the milestone — starts to tell you something real, something you can verify by simply looking at your own financial history with the dates lined up next to each other. This book will keep returning to that discipline: look at the timing, not just the event, and don't claim the mechanism until the pattern, not the single instance, has earned it.

It's worth being honest, early, about what this book is not claiming. It is not claiming that every large purchase after a windfall is self-sabotage, or that every loan to a family member is secretly a ceiling reflex in a trench coat, or that celebrating a win with something nice for yourself is evidence of a hidden psychological wound. Sometimes a boat is just a boat. Sometimes helping your sibling is just helping your sibling, full stop, no deeper mechanism required. This book is not asking you to pathologize every generous or celebratory decision you've ever made near a financial high point — that would be its own kind of trap, turning every joyful spend into a suspect one, which helps nobody and diagnoses everyone. What it is asking is narrower and more useful: to notice the pattern only when it repeats. One boat is a boat. A boat, then a bad loan eighteen months later at the next high point, then an uncharacteristic risky bet at the one after that — each one plausible on its own, each one arriving within weeks of a new peak — is not three unrelated events. It's a reflex with three data points, and the only way to see the reflex is to stop looking at the events one at a time and start looking at their timing relative to the number.

Each chapter ahead follows the same shape, because the shape is what makes the mechanism visible instead of theoretical. First, the pattern itself — a close, specific scene, someone at or just past a threshold, watching (though they wouldn't describe it this way in the moment) their own hand start to undo what they just built. A second scene from a different angle, so you can see the same mechanism operating at a different income level or through a different trigger — because the ceiling doesn't care whether the threshold is your first ten thousand dollars saved or your first million; the reflex is scale-independent, which is itself one of the most useful things to understand about it. Then the actual psychological mechanism underneath, named honestly, drawn from real research — self-verification theory, self-discrepancy theory, status quo bias, prospect theory, genuine work on self-sabotage — never invented, never dressed up to sound more authoritative than it is. Then the cost, counted in more than dollars. Then a set of overrides — real, specific things you can actually do, not vague encouragement to "shift your mindset." And a rule to carry forward, short enough to remember at the exact moment you'll need it, which is usually a moment that arrives fast and offers no warning.

Here is something worth sitting with before the chapters begin, because it will save you from a certain kind of confusion later: the ceiling is not a punishment and it's not a flaw in your character. It was, at the time it was installed, protective. A child who grows up in scarcity and learns that having "too much" draws danger, or envy, or the sudden withdrawal of a parent's love, is not being irrational when some part of them flags a large sum of money as a threat. A person raised in a family where wealth and belonging were fused develops, entirely sensibly given the evidence available to a child, an internal alarm that goes off whenever the numbers start to separate those two things. The ceiling was built by a much younger, much less resourced version of you, working with the only data that version had, trying to keep you safe inside a specific and often difficult set of circumstances. It did its job. The problem is that it never got the update. It's still running the original settings in a life that has changed completely, guarding a threshold that made sense at eight years old and makes no sense at all in the actual, adult, financially capable life you're now living. This book isn't about blaming the mechanism. It's about updating it.

It's worth being specific, too, about where this book's territory sits relative to the rest of your financial life, because "self-sabotage around money" is broad enough to mean a dozen different things depending on who's using the phrase. This book is not about spending habits in general, or about budgeting, or about the psychology of debt. It is specifically about what happens at the moment your finances exceed a felt-safe baseline — the earning and net-worth axis, not the day-to-day spending axis. You can have a perfectly ordinary relationship with your weekly grocery budget and still carry a ceiling that fires specifically and only at the level of raises, windfalls, and major milestones. The two are related but distinct, and this book has deliberately stayed narrow, because a book that tries to explain every possible way people relate badly to money ends up explaining none of them well. If what you're looking for is help with everyday spending discipline, this isn't quite the right volume. If what you're looking for is an explanation for why good financial news keeps mysteriously reversing itself, you're in the right place.

One more thing, and then we'll get into the specific shapes this takes. You are very likely going to recognize more than one of these chapters as your own. That's not a flaw in how the book is organized — it's how the ceiling actually operates. The same person can sabotage a raise through go-quiet negotiation avoidance and also blow past a savings milestone through a suspiciously timed purchase and also route money out through disguised generosity, because all three are the same underlying reflex finding whatever channel is available in that particular moment. The chapters are separated for clarity, not because real people confine themselves to one mechanism. Read for the ones that land, and don't be surprised if more than one does.

There is a reasonable question sitting underneath all of this, and it deserves a straight answer rather than a dodge: if the ceiling is unconscious, how can a book — words on a page, read once, maybe twice — actually change it? The honest answer is that reading alone won't. What reading can do, and what this book is built to do, is make the mechanism visible enough that you catch it in the act, in real time, the next time it fires — which is the only place it can actually be changed. You cannot argue with a reflex you don't know is happening. You can absolutely interrupt one you can name the instant you feel it start. That's the entire bet this book is making: not that insight alone rewires four decades of self-concept, but that insight plus a specific, practiced interruption, repeated across the next several ceilings you approach, slowly teaches your nervous system a new fact — that crossing the line doesn't produce the catastrophe it once implied it would. Each time you cross a threshold and don't reflexively bring the number back down, the old settings lose a little of their authority. The ceiling isn't erased in one reading. It's worn down, crossing by crossing, the same slow way it was built.

The number was never really about the number. It was about what having it would mean you'd have to believe about yourself — and whether the person you've quietly decided you are has room, in his or her self-concept, for that much. Everything from here is an argument for widening that room on purpose, deliberately, faster than your history would do it on its own. Let's start with where the ceiling actually gets built — not the moment you hit it, but the much earlier moment, usually long before you had any money at all, when a number first got installed as the edge of what you were allowed to have.

Chapter 1 — The Thermostat You Didn't Set

Picture a thermostat bolted to a wall in a house you didn't build, set to a temperature you didn't choose, by someone who died or moved out or simply stopped being present in your life decades ago. You've lived in this house so long you've forgotten the thermostat is even there — forgotten, really, that a house's temperature is a setting at all rather than just a fact about the world, like weather. And then one day you open a window on a warm afternoon, the room starts to warm up past the old setting, and without anyone touching a dial, the air conditioning kicks on. Cold air pours in until the room is back where it "should" be. You didn't do that. The system did. It was built to do exactly that, and it doesn't know the temperature it's defending is decades out of date.

This is the closest working image for what this book calls the ceiling: not a decision, not a belief you'd state out loud if asked, but a homeostatic setting — a thermostat for your sense of financial self — installed early, defended automatically, and largely invisible until you understand what you're looking at.

The rest of this book is about the specific ways that thermostat kicks the air conditioning on. But before any of that will make sense, you need to understand where the thermostat came from, who set it, and why a mechanism this costly persists at all when it seems to work directly against your own stated interests.

Notice, too, what the thermostat image gets right that a simpler metaphor — a ceiling you bump your head against, say — would miss. A physical ceiling is passive. You hit it, and it stops you, and that's the whole interaction. A thermostat is active. It doesn't merely stop you from rising; it actively works to bring you back down once you've risen, expending real effort in the process, the way an air conditioner runs a compressor rather than simply existing as an obstacle. That distinction matters enormously for what this book is arguing. This isn't a story about a limit you passively run into. It's a story about a system that notices you've exceeded a setting and then does something about it — which is exactly why the specific eight mechanisms in the chapters ahead exist at all. A passive ceiling would need no mechanisms; you'd simply stop rising. An active thermostat needs a whole toolkit of responses, deployed as needed, whichever one is available in the moment the room gets too warm. That toolkit is this book's subject.

Start with the psychology, because it's older and better established than most people realize, and it isn't fringe. In the 1980s, the psychologist William Swann formalized a body of research into what he called self-verification theory — the finding, replicated many times since, that people are motivated not simply to feel good about themselves, but to have the world confirm whatever they already believe about themselves, positive or negative. This sounds counterintuitive on first hearing — why would anyone seek confirmation of an unflattering self-belief? — but Swann's research found the drive is real and often stronger than the competing drive toward simple self-enhancement. A stable, confirmed identity, Swann's work suggests, feels safer than an accurate but destabilizing one, because a confirmed identity lets you predict your own life. You know, roughly, who you are, what happens to people like you, what to expect. An identity under active revision is a mind without a map, and minds without maps are, evolutionarily speaking, in more danger than minds with slightly wrong ones.

Swann's experiments found this held even for people with low self-esteem — participants who thought poorly of themselves would sometimes seek out partners and situations that confirmed the negative view, over more flattering alternatives, apparently preferring the stability of a bad-but-known story to the instability of a good-but-unfamiliar one.

Now apply that mechanism to money specifically. If somewhere in your self-concept — the working model you carry, mostly outside conscious awareness, of who you are — there is a figure, even a rough and unstated one, for how much money "someone like me" has, then your actual finances rising meaningfully above that figure doesn't register as pure good news to the self-verification system. It registers as a mismatch. The world is now telling you something about yourself — you have this much money — that contradicts what you already, more deeply, believe about yourself. And when self-concept and evidence disagree, the self-verification drive doesn't automatically update the self-concept to match the better evidence. Often, it does the opposite: it finds a way to bring the evidence back in line with the self-concept, because the self-concept is the thing doing the predicting, and predicting is the thing the whole system is built to protect. This is not a conscious process. Nobody sits down and decides, "I make more than I believe I deserve, so I will now find a way to lose some of it." It happens underneath language, the way a thermostat clicks on without anyone deciding, in the moment, that the room has gotten too warm.

A parallel body of research gives this mechanism an even more precise name where money is concerned. The psychologist E. Tory Higgins, building the self-discrepancy theory referenced elsewhere in this library, distinguished between your actual self — who your circumstances currently say you are — and other internalized reference points, including what he called the "ought self": who you believe, at a near-instinctive level, you're supposed to be, based on standards absorbed early, often from caregivers, often before you were old enough to evaluate whether those standards made sense. A discrepancy between your actual self and your ought self produces a specific emotional signature — agitation, unease, a free-floating sense that something is wrong — even when, viewed from outside, nothing is wrong at all. If your "ought self" was calibrated in a household where money was scarce, or dangerous, or morally suspect, or fused with a parent's approval in ways that felt conditional and precarious, then earning meaningfully more than that ought-self ceiling doesn't feel like arrival. It feels like drift — like you've wandered somewhere you don't have standing to be, and the agitation that follows isn't really about the money at all. It's the discrepancy alarm, doing exactly what it evolved to do: flagging the gap between the self you're supposed to be and the self the evidence now describes, so that something can be done to close it.

Here is where the mechanism gets its teeth, and where it stops being an abstract psychological curiosity and starts costing people real, countable money. Closing a discrepancy can happen two ways. The self-concept can update to match the new, better evidence — which is slow, effortful, and often actively resisted, because updating a self-concept that's been stable for decades feels destabilizing even when the update is good news. Or the evidence can be brought back down to match the old self-concept — which is fast, requires no conscious insight at all, and can be accomplished through any of a thousand plausible-looking financial decisions that nobody, including the person making them, would recognize in the moment as a correction. An impulsive purchase. A loan given too fast, to someone who won't repay it, out of a generosity that feels selfless but functions as a release valve. A negotiation quietly sabotaged before it can conclude. A risky bet that has no real strategic logic behind it, made by someone who is otherwise careful with money in every other domain of their life. Every chapter that follows in this book is one specific shape this correction takes. They look different from the outside — a boat purchase looks nothing like a stalled salary negotiation, which looks nothing like an ill-timed loan to a sibling — but underneath, they're the same maneuver: the fastest available route back to a number that feels correct, deployed by a system that experiences the old number as safety and the new number as an error to be fixed.

It's worth pausing on a related and slightly different mechanism, because the two often travel together and get confused for each other. Status quo bias — documented by the economists William Samuelson and Richard Zeckhauser in a landmark 1988 paper — describes a separate but compounding tendency: people display a strong, largely irrational preference for the current state of affairs simply because it's current, independent of whether a change would objectively improve their position. Samuelson and Zeckhauser found this bias operating even in decisions with no emotional weight attached — retirement plan defaults, insurance options — where the "current" choice was sticky purely because it was already the choice, not because anyone had actively evaluated and preferred it. Layer that onto a financial ceiling and the picture sharpens: it isn't only that your old, lower number feels correct in some deep identity sense. It's that your old, lower number is also simply *familiar*, and familiarity itself exerts its own separate gravitational pull, entirely apart from whatever your ought-self believes you deserve. Self-discrepancy explains why the higher number feels like an error. Status quo bias explains why, once an error has been flagged, the fastest correction available is always the one that returns you to the state you already know, rather than forward into a new and unfamiliar one you've never actually occupied before.

It's worth pausing on where, specifically, this thermostat setting tends to get installed, because "childhood" is accurate but too vague to be useful on its own. The research on early money socialization — including the money scripts framework developed by Brad and Ted Klontz, referenced elsewhere in this library — points to a narrower window than most people assume: the majority of a person's core beliefs about money are formed before the age of seven, often through observation rather than instruction, absorbed from the emotional register surrounding money in the household rather than from any explicit lesson. A child doesn't need to be told "we don't have money for that" to absorb a scarcity ceiling. They need only watch a parent's shoulders tighten at the mail, or notice that certain topics get a door closed on them at dinner, or feel the specific quality of relief in a room when a bill turns out to be smaller than feared. None of that is a lesson in the conventional sense. It's atmosphere, and atmosphere installs beliefs far more durably than direct instruction does, precisely because atmosphere never announces itself as a belief being taught — it just becomes, over enough repetition, the water a child assumes everyone swims in.

This is worth naming plainly because it explains something that otherwise looks contradictory: people who grew up genuinely poor and people who grew up genuinely comfortable both develop ceilings, and at first glance that seems to undercut the idea that scarcity is the driving force. It isn't, exactly — scarcity is one common origin, but not the only one. A child raised in real financial hardship may install a ceiling that says, roughly, "people like us don't have this much, and having it would be dangerous or dishonest somehow." A child raised in wealth, but in a household where money was the primary currency of parental approval or the source of constant tension between parents, may install an entirely different ceiling — one that says "money is where the conflict lives" or "money is how love gets measured, and I'm not sure I can sustain being measured at that level forever." Both ceilings limit adult financial behavior in strikingly similar ways despite originating from opposite material conditions, because the mechanism was never really about the amount of money present in the house. It was about what money came to represent emotionally inside that house — danger, conflict, conditional love, instability — and representations, once installed, don't check your current bank balance before they fire.

There's a third common origin worth naming alongside scarcity and fused approval, because it doesn't require either extreme and probably describes the largest number of readers: simple, ordinary calibration to whatever income and net worth surrounded you growing up, with no drama attached to it at all. A person raised in a comfortably middle-class household, with no particular scarcity trauma and no particular wealth-as-love fusion, still absorbs, passively and continuously, a working sense of what a "normal" amount of money looks like — a number implicitly calibrated to the neighborhood, the school, the friends' families, the general financial atmosphere of that specific childhood. Exceeding that ordinary, undramatic baseline as an adult can trigger the identical discomfort as exceeding a scarcity-driven or approval-driven ceiling, even though nothing about the original calibration involved any hardship or conflict at all. The thermostat doesn't require trauma to install a setting. It only requires years of consistent exposure to one particular number as the norm, which is true of essentially everyone's childhood, regardless of how emotionally uneventful that childhood was.

It helps to see the thermostat caught in the act, once, before the book moves into its eight specific shapes, because an abstract mechanism is easy to nod along with and easy to forget. A woman in her late twenties, newly promoted into her first management role, describes to a friend, almost as a joke, a strange ritual she's noticed in herself: every time her checking account crosses a certain figure — not a huge number, just a specific one that seems to matter to her for reasons she can't articulate — she finds herself, within a week, booking something. A trip, usually. Nothing reckless, nothing that would alarm anyone looking at her bank statement in isolation. Just enough, each time, to bring the number back under the line. She tells this story lightly, as a quirk, the way people describe always needing to reorganize their desk before starting a big project. She has never once connected it to anything about her childhood, her self-concept, or a threshold her nervous system quietly defends. She experiences it, entirely sincerely, as liking to travel. And she does like to travel — that part is true. What she hasn't yet noticed is the timing, because nobody has ever handed her a reason to look for it. That's the gap this book exists to close: not to tell her she doesn't really like travel, but to show her the pattern sitting underneath a genuine preference, quietly recruiting it, again and again, on a schedule that has nothing to do with wanderlust and everything to do with a number on a screen.

None of this means the ceiling is destiny, and it's worth saying that plainly here, at the start, because it will matter for every chapter that follows: a thermostat is a setting, not a law of physics. Settings can be changed. They don't change themselves, and they rarely change from insight alone — you cannot simply decide, once, in a moment of clarity, that your ceiling is now higher, and expect the reflex to comply the next time real money arrives. But settings that are named, watched for, and deliberately overridden at the exact moment they try to fire, again and again, across enough repetitions, do move.

It's worth being specific about the mechanics of that movement, because "settings can be changed" is easy to say and vague enough to be useless without a model of how the change actually happens. A thermostat's setting isn't changed by staring at it, or by feeling strongly that it should be different, or by reading a persuasive argument for why seventy-four degrees is a perfectly reasonable temperature. It's changed by someone physically moving the dial, repeatedly, until the new setting becomes the one the system defends instead of the old one. Applied to a financial ceiling, the "dial" is behavioral, not cognitive: it's the actual, lived experience of crossing a threshold and staying there, unpunished, long enough for the nervous system to update its model of what's survivable. Reading this book moves you toward the dial. It doesn't turn it. Only the repeated, deliberate act of crossing a threshold and not letting the reflex correct it — the specific overrides in each of the following chapters — actually turns it, one crossing at a time, the way a hand actually turns a physical dial one degree at a time rather than all at once.

That's the entire operating premise of the eight chapters ahead. Each one takes a different shape this reflex wears — the impulse purchase timed to a windfall, the stalled negotiation, the disguised generosity, the reckless bet, the sabotaged deal, and others — and does the same four things to it: shows you the pattern closely enough that you recognize your own life in it, names the actual mechanism (never invented, always attributable to real, citable research), counts what it actually costs you beyond the dollar figure, and hands you real, specific things to do differently the next time you feel the pull.

You will likely recognize yourself in more than one chapter. That's expected, not a sign you're unusually afflicted — the ceiling doesn't confine itself to a single channel per person, because the underlying reflex is the same regardless of which specific behavior happens to be available in a given moment. Someone who stalls their own salary negotiations may also, in a different context, make an uncharacteristically reckless investment right after a business milestone; both are the identical thermostat, defending the identical old temperature, through whichever door happens to be open. Read for the chapters that land the hardest. Don't be surprised if it's more than one, and don't take that as evidence you're somehow more broken than average — it's evidence the mechanism is doing exactly what it was built to do, consistently, across every domain where it can reach.

It's worth naming, too, why the specific channel varies from person to person and even from threshold to threshold within the same person's life, because that variability isn't random. The channel the reflex reaches for tends to follow whatever release valve is most available and least scrutinized in a given context — someone with a business partner watching closely might find the reckless bet harder to execute unnoticed, and drift instead toward the quieter, more private discount they keep giving their own rates. Someone whose family constantly asks for financial help might find the generous leak the path of least resistance, simply because the opportunity to give is already sitting right there, pre-justified, the moment the discomfort arrives. The mechanism is opportunistic, not fixed. It doesn't commit to one costume for life. It uses whatever door happens to be unlocked and unwatched in a given season of your life, which is exactly why learning to recognize the underlying shape — rather than memorizing a single behavior to watch for — matters more than any individual chapter's specific scenario.

This also explains why the same person's channel can shift across their own lifetime, even without any conscious decision to change tactics. Someone early in a career, with modest savings and no business partner or spouse yet watching closely, might find the alarm purchase or the reckless bet the easiest available door — private, fast, requiring no one else's awareness. The same person, a decade later, married, running a business, more publicly visible, might find those same doors far harder to use unnoticed, and drift instead toward the quieter mechanisms — the discount they keep giving themselves, the visibility they keep declining — simply because those doors remain open to scrutiny in ways the earlier ones no longer are. The reflex doesn't mature or evolve in any meaningful sense. It just keeps finding the path of least resistance, wherever that path happens to be at each stage of a life that keeps changing shape around it.

Here is the rule this whole book stands on, worth carrying forward as you read everything that follows: the ceiling was never a judgment about how much money you deserve. It was a thermostat setting installed by a younger self working with old information, and old information can be updated the moment you're willing to look directly at where the setting actually came from — which is the work of every chapter from here forward.

Chapter 2 — The Alarm Purchase

Why the Money Doesn't Feel Safe Until You've Spent Some of It

The savings app shows a number she's never seen before, and her first feeling isn't pride. It's a kind of static.

She's thirty-four, a physical therapist who has spent six years building this account one automatic transfer at a time, watching it climb in increments so small they were barely visible week to week. Tonight, for the first time, the number crosses a threshold she'd privately set as a marker years ago without ever writing it down anywhere — a round number, the kind you pick as a kid deciding what "rich" means before you have any real information to calibrate it with. She stares at the screen for a long moment, waiting for the feeling she assumed would arrive. It doesn't. What arrives instead is a low, wordless hum of wrongness, the specific unease of information that doesn't fit the story you've been telling yourself. She closes the app. She goes to bed. She doesn't mention it to anyone.

Four days later, she buys a car. Not the sensible used sedan she'd been comparing spreadsheets on for eight months — a newer one, nicer than she needs, financed at a rate she didn't shop around for, purchased in a single afternoon with a speed that surprises even her. She tells herself, and later tells her sister, that she'd "earned it," that six years of discipline deserved a reward, that the timing was coincidental — the old car had been making a noise, after all. All of that is true. None of it explains why the decision took ninety minutes from browsing to signature, a speed utterly unlike every other financial choice she's made in the six years it took to build the account she just, in effect, partially undid. The savings total, after the down payment and the new monthly payment carved out of her budget, settles back down near — not exactly at, but close enough to feel like a landing — the number just below the one that had made her so uneasy four nights earlier.

A software developer in his late twenties runs the same program at a different scale and through a different door. He's just received his first equity payout after a company acquisition — not life-changing money, but more than he's ever held at once, more than either of his parents made in a year growing up. He doesn't buy anything large. Instead, over the following three weeks, he loses a meaningful chunk of it in a series of speculative trades on volatile assets he doesn't actually understand, made with a carelessness that would embarrass the version of him who spends hours reviewing pull requests for a stray semicolon. He'd tell you, if you asked in the moment, that he was "diversifying" or "trying to grow it faster." He would not tell you — because he doesn't know it — that the trades started the same week the payout cleared, and that by the time the losses stopped, the number in his account had drifted back down to something close to what he'd have called normal a month earlier. Different vehicle, identical destination.

A retired schoolteacher in her early sixties offers a third version of the same shape, at a scale and pace that make the mechanism almost comically visible in hindsight. She inherits a modest sum from an aunt she wasn't especially close to — enough to meaningfully pad a retirement that had, until that point, felt tight in a way she'd quietly worried about for years. For the first two weeks, she does nothing, uncertain what to do with a number this size arriving all at once. Then, over a single weekend, she redoes her kitchen — not a modest refresh, a full renovation, cabinets and countertops and a farmhouse sink she'd pinned to a board years ago and never seriously priced out. The contractor she hires is the first one who returns her call, no comparison quotes gathered, no negotiation attempted, an urgency to the whole undertaking that surprises her daughter, who has never known her mother to make a purchase over two hundred dollars without at least a week of deliberation. By the time the renovation is paid for, the inheritance and the retirement cushion it was meant to pad are, for practical purposes, the same account they were before her aunt died. She'll tell you, and mean it, that she'd always wanted that kitchen. She's right. She'd also always wanted, more than the kitchen, to never have to think about her retirement account again — and forty-eight hours after the money that could have finally delivered that arrived, some part of her made sure it wouldn't.

Three weeks after the car purchase, the physical therapist sits at her kitchen table with the loan paperwork spread out, running numbers she hadn't fully run before signing. The monthly payment, next to her actual budget, is tighter than she let herself notice in the dealership showroom, where the whole transaction had a kind of forward momentum that made stopping to recalculate feel almost rude. She doesn't regret the car exactly — she likes driving it, genuinely — but she notices, filling out a line on a spreadsheet she still keeps out of habit, that the savings total has settled into a range that feels, for lack of a better word, normal again. She doesn't consciously connect this to relief. She just notices that the static from that first night — the hum of wrongness she felt looking at the new, higher number — isn't there anymore, replaced by something closer to familiarity. She has no language yet for what just happened. She only has the spreadsheet, and the quiet.

What's actually happening

Neither of these people is impulsive by nature. That's the detail worth sitting with before anything else, because it's the detail that makes this pattern so hard to see in yourself: the alarm purchase doesn't look like a character flaw, because the person making it isn't, in every other domain, someone who makes fast, unresearched, financially significant decisions. The physical therapist spent six years being careful. The developer reviews code for a living. The speed and carelessness are not personality traits leaking out. They're evidence that something has temporarily overridden the person's normal decision-making process — and the timing, arriving within days of a threshold crossing, is the clue to what that something is.

This is self-verification theory again, but seen from its behavioral side rather than its cognitive one. William Swann's research, discussed in the previous chapter, established that people are motivated to keep the world confirming their existing self-concept — but Swann and later researchers also documented the mechanics of *how* that confirmation gets restored when it's threatened. It isn't always passive. Sometimes people actively behave in ways that produce the confirming evidence, essentially manufacturing the outcome their self-concept expects, because manufactured confirmation resolves the discomfort of discrepancy faster than waiting for the world to somehow revert on its own. If your self-concept has, embedded in it since childhood, a working idea of "how much money someone like me realistically holds," and your actual balance drifts meaningfully above that figure, one of the fastest available routes back to psychological equilibrium is to make the balance smaller again — through any decision that's fast, plausible, and doesn't require you to consciously admit what you're doing. A car. A trade. Something real, something defensible in conversation, something that never once has to be named, even privately, as a correction.

It's worth pausing on why the alarm purchase specifically, rather than some other release valve, is often the first mechanism a person's ceiling reaches for, because the answer says something important about how automatic this process actually is. An alarm purchase requires no negotiation with anyone else, no waiting period, no third party who might ask an uncomfortable question about timing. It's a private transaction between a person and their own discomfort, executable in minutes, leaving behind a plausible artifact — a car, a device, a trip — that provides its own built-in cover story. Compare that to the mechanisms in later chapters: sabotaging a deal requires a deal in progress; giving money away requires someone to give it to; a stalled negotiation requires a negotiation to stall. The alarm purchase requires nothing except access to a bank account and a store, which is to say it requires nothing at all, which is exactly why it tends to be the reflex's fastest and most frequently used channel, especially for anyone whose ceiling gets triggered by a savings milestone rather than an earned windfall tied to a specific negotiation or relationship.

There's a useful parallel from a completely different domain of psychology that clarifies why this feels less like a decision and more like relief. Homeostasis is usually discussed in physiology — the body's automatic correction of temperature, blood sugar, hydration back toward a set point whenever it drifts too far in either direction — but psychologists have long used the same framework to describe how self-concept behaves under threat: as a system defending a set point, not a system that simply floats wherever new evidence takes it. A number too far below the set point produces distress recognizable as inadequacy, familiar to anyone who's felt bad about underearning. But a number too far *above* the set point produces its own distinct distress — less discussed, less socially legible, and easy to misread as something else entirely, because "I have too much money and it's making me anxious" is not a sentence most people have permission to say out loud, even to themselves. The alarm purchase is the discharge of that second, less legible distress. It isn't the pursuit of pleasure. It's the pursuit of a familiar number, wearing pleasure's clothes.

How to tell the difference. Not every purchase after a windfall is an alarm purchase, and it's worth being rigorous about the distinction before you start relabeling your own history. An ordinary celebratory purchase tends to share three features: it was, to some extent, already planned or wanted before the money arrived; its size is proportionate to the milestone, not suspiciously close to erasing it entirely; and the decision, even if made quickly, doesn't produce that specific, wordless static beforehand — the sense of wrongness that precedes the purchase rather than following it. An alarm purchase, by contrast, tends to arrive with little or no prior planning, lands with unusual precision near the exact amount needed to bring the balance back under the old threshold, and is preceded by a period of genuine discomfort that the purchase then visibly, immediately resolves. The physical therapist's car checked every box in the second category. A modest, previously-planned vacation booked with an unchanged mood beforehand and an unchanged mood afterward would not have. The test isn't the dollar amount. It's the shape of the discomfort before, and the specific quality of relief after.

What it costs you

The dollar cost is the easiest to count and, as always, the least important part. A car bought in ninety minutes instead of eight months of research typically comes at a real premium — a worse rate, a worse trade-in value, options paid for that weren't actually wanted, all because speed was the point, not the vehicle. The developer's speculative losses are simpler still: money that existed, and now doesn't, spent chasing a feeling of familiarity rather than a return. But dollar cost, again, understates the real damage, because the real damage is what the pattern does to the next threshold.

Every time an alarm purchase successfully brings the number back down, it doesn't just cost the specific dollar amount spent. It reinforces the entire mechanism — teaches the system, at a level below language, that this is what happens when the number gets too high, that discomfort followed by a fast plausible purchase followed by relief is the correct and reliable sequence. The next threshold arrives with the pattern more deeply grooved than the last one, not less. Meanwhile, the actual project the money was for — the house down payment, the runway for starting a business, the retirement cushion — never accumulates past the old ceiling, year after year, threshold after threshold, no matter how much is earned in between. The person doesn't experience this as failure to save. They experience it as a series of unrelated, individually reasonable purchases. The pattern is invisible from inside any single instance of it. It's only visible in aggregate, looking back across several years at the specific timing of when the "reasonable" purchases happened to land.

There's a compounding structural cost worth naming specifically, because it's easy to underweight if you only think in terms of a single missed threshold: every dollar redirected into an alarm purchase is a dollar that doesn't get the chance to compound. Money sitting in savings or invested is money doing quiet, invisible work over years and decades; money spent on a car depreciating in a driveway is not. The physical therapist's decision doesn't just cost her the difference between the car she needed and the car she bought. Over a thirty-year horizon, at any reasonable rate of return, it costs her a multiple of that difference — money that will never get the chance to become retirement security, because it got redirected at the exact moment it crossed into a range that made her uneasy. The ceiling doesn't just cap a number. It caps the compounding that number would otherwise have been doing on your behalf, silently, for decades, without you ever having to think about it again.

The schoolteacher's kitchen renovation carries a cost worth naming for its own specific reason: inheritances and windfalls are, for most people, rare and unrepeatable events, which makes an alarm purchase against one particularly expensive in relative terms. A raise or a business milestone can, in principle, happen again next year, giving a person another chance to catch the pattern the next time around. An inheritance from a specific relative happens exactly once. The retirement cushion her aunt's death could have meaningfully padded is not coming back around for a second attempt, which means the cost of this particular alarm purchase isn't just the money itself — it's the loss of what may have been her one real opportunity to close a gap she'd quietly worried about for years, replaced instead with a kitchen she'll enjoy, genuinely, for the fifteen or twenty years she has left in that house, while the worry about her retirement account returns, unaddressed, within a season.

The overrides

Name the threshold before you reach it. Most people have never consciously identified their internal ceiling number, which means they can't recognize themselves approaching it. Take five minutes and write down, honestly, the first number that comes to mind when you ask yourself, "What amount would start to feel like too much?" You may be surprised how quickly and specifically an answer arrives — that speed is itself information, evidence the number has been sitting there, unexamined, for longer than you realized.

Install a 72-hour rule specifically for the week after a financial high point. Not for all purchases, forever — a blanket rule like that rarely survives contact with real life. Specifically for any purchase over a threshold you set for yourself, made within two weeks of crossing a new financial high point. The alarm purchase depends on speed; speed is what lets it bypass your normal judgment. Seventy-two hours of mandatory waiting doesn't prevent the purchase if it's genuinely a good idea. It just removes the reflex's only real weapon.

The Move: the next time you cross a threshold, do nothing with the money for one full week, and notice the discomfort without acting on it. Don't spend it, don't move it, don't "put it to work" — just let it sit, exactly where it is, and pay attention to what you feel. Most people have never simply held the discomfort of a higher number without immediately discharging it through action. The feeling will likely be real — restlessness, a nagging sense that something needs to be done, maybe even something close to guilt. Let it be there without obeying it. This is the single most direct way to prove to your own nervous system that the number can stay elevated without anything catastrophic happening, which is the exact belief the alarm purchase exists to prevent you from ever testing.

Track your own threshold history before the next one arrives. Look back across the last two or three times your finances made a meaningful jump — a raise, a bonus, a savings milestone — and write down what happened financially in the four weeks after each one. Most people have never done this exercise, because each instance felt, at the time, like an isolated and reasonable decision. Lined up together, with dates attached, the pattern is often obvious in a way no single instance ever was. This isn't about guilt. It's about giving yourself the same evidence a outside observer would have, since an outside observer is precisely what your own judgment can't be in the moment the alarm is firing.

Separate the reward from the removal. If part of what's driving the purchase is a genuine, legitimate desire to celebrate a milestone — and often it is, tangled up with the reflex rather than separate from it — give yourself the celebration without giving yourself the removal. Take the trip, buy the smaller version of the thing, mark the moment. Just do it at a scale that doesn't return the account to its old resting number. You're allowed to enjoy what you built. You're not obligated to also dismantle it in the same gesture.

For sudden, unearned-feeling windfalls specifically — an inheritance, a settlement, a gift — build in a mandatory delay before any large decision. The schoolteacher's inheritance moved from arrival to full renovation in a single weekend, with no comparison quotes and no real deliberation, precisely because money that arrives without ongoing effort attached to it feels less like "hers" and more like something to be quickly converted into something tangible before it can somehow slip away. A fixed rule — thirty days, minimum, before any purchase over a set threshold, for any money that arrived through inheritance, settlement, or gift specifically — counters this directly, because the urgency the reflex manufactures rarely survives even a modest, pre-committed waiting period.

It's worth returning, briefly, to the physical therapist and the developer one more time, because the way their stories actually resolved says something hopeful about how quickly this pattern can loosen once it's been named. The physical therapist, months after the car purchase, crosses a new, higher threshold — larger than the first one, in fact, since her income has grown in the interim. She feels the same static she felt before. This time, having read something that put language to the feeling for the first time, she recognizes it, waits the week, and doesn't buy anything. The number stays elevated. Nothing catastrophic happens. She describes the experience afterward as anticlimactic, almost boring — which is exactly the point. The alarm purchase thrives on the belief that the discomfort is unbearable and must be resolved immediately. The single most effective treatment turns out to be discovering, directly and in your own body, that it wasn't.

The schoolteacher, years later, receives a second, smaller inheritance from a different relative. This time, having finally connected the earlier kitchen renovation to the pattern this book describes, she gives herself the thirty-day rule before deciding anything. The urgency she remembers from before — the specific, pressing sense that something needed to be done with the money immediately — arrives again, right on schedule, and this time she simply notices it rather than obeying it. By day thirty, the urgency has faded on its own, the way urgency generally does when nothing feeds it. She adds the full amount to her retirement account, the exact account the first inheritance was quietly diverted away from, and feels, for the first time in years, something closer to relief than dread when she checks its balance.

The number was never the danger. The relief of bringing it back down was — because relief that comes from losing ground is the clearest signal available that a ceiling, not a decision, just made your choice for you.

Chapter 3 — The Ask You Didn't Make

Why the Sabotage Sometimes Happens Before the Money Even Arrives

She's rehearsed the conversation in the shower, in the car, twice out loud to her dog. She has the market data. She has the list of projects that shipped under budget and ahead of schedule because of decisions she personally made. She has, printed and folded in her bag, a number that isn't even aggressive — a number her own research says she's underpaid relative to, a number her manager would almost certainly approve without much of a fight. She has fifteen minutes on the calendar with that manager, block-titled, deliberately vague, "Quick check-in."

The fifteen minutes happen. She talks about a project timeline. She mentions, in passing, that things have been going well. Her manager agrees, warmly, genuinely. There is a natural, open pause — the exact pause she rehearsed walking into — where the sentence she's practiced fifty times is supposed to go. She says, instead, "Anyway, just wanted to touch base," and stands up. She is in the hallway before she fully registers what just happened. She will tell herself, walking back to her desk, that the timing wasn't quite right, that she'll bring it up next quarter when the current project wraps, that she doesn't want to seem like she's only in it for the money. She has told herself some version of this for three consecutive review cycles.

A restaurant owner runs the identical program in a completely different register. His restaurant, after four difficult years, has finally found its footing — reviews are strong, tables are full most nights, and for the first time he's in a position to raise prices to a level that actually reflects his costs and his margins, a change every advisor and every fellow owner he trusts has told him is not just reasonable but overdue. He drafts the new menu. He sets a date. The date arrives, and he tells his kitchen manager to "hold off a bit longer, let's not rock the boat while things are going well." Three months later, the date arrives again, self-imposed, and gets pushed again — this time because a slightly slow Tuesday made him nervous, a single data point he wouldn't have weighted at all six months earlier when the restaurant was actually struggling and every data point mattered. The prices never change. The restaurant keeps running at a margin that quietly caps how much he can ever pay himself, no matter how full the tables get.

A freelance illustrator in her mid-thirties runs a quieter, slower-motion version of the same pattern, one that takes years rather than weeks to become visible. A publisher she's worked with for a long time offers her, unprompted, a significantly larger project — a full book cover series instead of the single spot illustrations she's always done for them, at a rate that would roughly triple what she's ever earned from a single client relationship. She says she'll think about it. She thinks about it, genuinely, for eleven months, asking for one clarification after another, none of which meaningfully changes her assessment of the opportunity, each one simply buying another few weeks before she has to actually answer. The publisher, patient at first, eventually assumes silence means no and quietly moves the project to another illustrator. She finds out from a mutual friend, months later, feels a genuine pang of loss, and tells herself it probably wasn't the right time anyway, her plate was full, she wasn't sure she could deliver at that scope reliably. None of that was false. All of it was also, transparently, a series of reasons generated after the fact to explain a decision that was never really about scheduling at all.

What's actually happening

This chapter's version of the ceiling is worth distinguishing carefully from Chapter 2's, because the mechanism fires at a different point in the sequence and looks, from the outside, almost like its opposite. The alarm purchase happens after the money arrives, correcting a number that already changed. The stalled ask happens before the money arrives at all, preventing the number from ever having to change in the first place. Same thermostat. Different strategy for defending the same set point — and in some ways, this version is the more efficient one, because it never has to spend anything to work. It just has to make sure the conversation doesn't happen, or happens too softly to land, or gets rescheduled one more time.

The psychological literature on approach-avoidance conflict, developed initially by Kurt Lewin and extended by decades of subsequent research, describes exactly this shape: a goal that is simultaneously desired and threatening produces a distinct behavioral signature, where a person moves toward the goal with real effort and preparation right up until they're close enough that the threatening quality of the goal starts to outweigh its pull, at which point they stall, retreat, or find a plausible reason to not quite arrive. What makes a raise or a price increase threatening, when it's also clearly desired, is exactly the self-discrepancy mechanism from Chapter 1: the new number, if it lands, will require updating a self-concept that's been stable for years, possibly decades. The fifteen minutes in the office aren't just a conversation about compensation. They're the doorway into a version of the self-concept that includes "the kind of person who earns this much" — and standing in that doorway, close enough to feel the threshold underfoot, is precisely where the avoidance half of the conflict gets loudest. She doesn't fail to make the ask because she's afraid of rejection, exactly, though that's the story she'd tell herself. She stalls because some part of her recognizes that success is the more destabilizing outcome of the two.

It's worth noticing, too, what makes this particular version of the ceiling so much harder to catch than the alarm purchase from the previous chapter. An alarm purchase leaves a receipt — an artifact you can look back on and eventually connect to a date. A stalled ask leaves nothing at all. There's no transaction to trace, no statement line to notice months later, no moment where the absence of a raise shows up as a debit. It just shows up as a number that never grew the way it could have, indistinguishable, on paper, from a hundred ordinary reasons a raise might not have happened — market conditions, a tight budget year, a manager who simply never got around to it. The stalled ask is the version of the ceiling that hides most easily behind circumstances outside your control, which is exactly why it's worth being unusually rigorous about noticing your own role in it, since nobody else is likely to point it out to you.

The illustrator's eleven-month delay is worth returning to here, because it shows a subtler variant of the same mechanism, stretched across a timeline long enough that even she never experienced it as a single decision. Each individual clarifying question she asked the publisher was reasonable in isolation — a fair question about deadlines, a fair question about creative control, a fair question about kill fees. Approach-avoidance conflict doesn't always resolve in one dramatic retreat, the way it did for the woman who stood up mid-conversation with her manager. Sometimes it resolves through a long, respectable-looking sequence of genuine due diligence that never quite concludes, each question buying a small amount of additional distance from the threshold without ever requiring the person to consciously decide they're avoiding it. The stall doesn't always look like fifteen minutes in an office. Sometimes it looks like eleven months of thoroughness that, examined honestly, thoroughness alone doesn't explain.

There is a further wrinkle specific to this chapter worth naming on its own, because it explains why the restaurant owner's stall looks so reasonable in the moment. Behavioral economists have long documented loss aversion — the finding, central to Daniel Kahneman and Amos Tversky's prospect theory, that losses are experienced roughly twice as intensely as equivalent gains. Most people apply this only to money already held: losing a hundred dollars hurts more than gaining a hundred dollars feels good. But the same asymmetry applies to identity. Once someone has stabilized around a self-concept — "a restaurant that's finally breaking even, run by someone who's careful and doesn't take big swings" — the *loss* of that specific, hard-won stability, even in service of a clearly better outcome, registers more powerfully than the *gain* of the better outcome itself. Raising prices doesn't just risk a slow Tuesday. It risks losing the identity of "the guy who kept this place afloat through the hard years by being careful," an identity that took four difficult years to earn and that a single price increase, however sound the math, feels like it could unravel. The math says raise the prices. The loss-aversion math, running underneath the conscious math, says protect the story you've already paid so much to build.

How to tell the difference. Not every unmade ask is a ceiling reflex. Sometimes the timing genuinely is wrong — a company going through real layoffs, a restaurant in a neighborhood actually experiencing a temporary downturn — and deferring the conversation is sound judgment rather than avoidance wearing judgment's clothes. The distinguishing test is recurrence and readiness: has this specific ask been prepared, rehearsed, and stood at the threshold of more than once, with a new plausible reason arriving each time the threshold is reached? A single deferral for a documented, external reason is ordinary caution. A pattern of near-identical preparation followed by near-identical last-second retreat, across multiple attempts, months or years apart, each with its own freshly-generated reasonable excuse, is the signature this chapter describes. If you can point to one external, verifiable fact that changed the calculus each time, trust your judgment. If the reason feels freshly invented in the moment and slightly different each time despite the underlying facts staying the same, that's worth a second, more skeptical look.

What it costs you

The dollar cost compounds in the most literal way possible: a raise not asked for, a price increase not implemented, doesn't just cost the difference for one pay cycle or one season. It resets the baseline every future increase gets calculated from. The physical therapist in the previous chapter loses a specific purchase's worth of money each time the alarm fires. The person who stalls the ask loses a baseline — every future negotiation, every future menu revision, starts from a number lower than it should have, indefinitely, because raises are usually calculated as a percentage of a starting figure, and a stalled ask keeps quietly discounting that starting figure for years after the original moment has been forgotten.

The harder cost to see is what stalling does to the story the person tells about their own agency. Each postponed ask gets filed, consciously, under a reasonable-sounding excuse — bad timing, not wanting to seem greedy, waiting for the right moment. But some part of the person knows, underneath the excuse, that the moment was right and they didn't take it, and that knowledge accumulates as a specific, quiet erosion of self-trust. Not "I'm bad at negotiating," which would at least be a specific, fixable skill gap. Something closer to "I don't actually go after things, even when I've prepared, even when I'm right." That's a heavier verdict to carry than a missed raise, and it tends to make the next ask even harder to make, because now there's a track record of stalling working against the attempt before it's even begun.

There's a compounding cost specific to the restaurant owner's version of this pattern worth naming, because it shows how a stalled ask can quietly cap an entire enterprise rather than just one person's paycheck. Every employee on his payroll, every future hire, every investment back into the restaurant's equipment or staff or physical space, is constrained by a margin he's chosen, repeatedly, not to correct. The stalled price increase isn't just costing him personally. It's costing the business's entire capacity to grow, because a restaurant that can't pay itself a sustainable margin can't reinvest, can't weather a slow season without panic, can't offer raises to the staff who've stayed loyal through the hard years he's so protective of. The ceiling, in a business context, doesn't cap one person's number. It caps everyone downstream of that number too.

The illustrator's eleven-month stall carries a cost specific to creative and relationship-based work worth naming on its own: reputational capital that decays if unused. The publisher didn't just move on to another illustrator for one project. They updated, quietly and probably permanently, their internal sense of who to call first for major work — a recalibration that happens below the level of any explicit conversation, the same way a client stops thinking of a contractor as "the person for the big jobs" after enough missed windows, without ever articulating the shift even to themselves. The illustrator's skill didn't change. Her position in that publisher's mental roster did, and repositioning back to where she was before the stall, if it's even fully possible, will take considerably longer than the eleven months it took to lose the standing in the first place. Trust compounds slowly and erodes fast, and a stalled ask spends down exactly the kind of trust that's hardest to rebuild.

The overrides

Separate the preparation from the delivery, and notice which one you're actually avoiding. Most people who stall the ask are excellent at the preparation — they've done the research, built the case, rehearsed the words. The avoidance lives entirely in the final step, the actual moment of speech. Naming this precisely matters, because it means the fix isn't "get better at negotiating." You're already good at that part. The fix is specifically at the delivery threshold, which is a much narrower and more addressable target.

Remove the option to reschedule yourself. If you notice a pattern of self-initiated postponement — "I'll bring it up next quarter," "let's not rock the boat right now" — take the decision about timing out of your own hands. Tell a colleague, a partner, or a coach the specific date you're going to make the ask, out loud, in advance, to a person who will actually follow up. The stall thrives in private, where a postponement costs nothing but a quiet inner negotiation with yourself. It survives much less easily once someone else is going to ask how it went.

The Move: schedule the ask for the earliest available moment after you're ready, not the moment that feels emotionally comfortable. There will never be a version of this conversation that feels fully comfortable — that comfort is not coming, and waiting for it is functionally identical to waiting forever, because the discomfort isn't about timing, it's about the identity threshold on the other side of the conversation. Pick the earliest realistic date once your preparation is genuinely done, put it on the calendar, and treat "I don't feel ready" as background noise rather than new information, because by the time you're this prepared, the feeling of unreadiness is the ceiling talking, not an accurate read of your actual case.

Notice the specific sentence you reach for in the pause, and interrupt it by name. Almost everyone who stalls an ask has a go-to line they reach for in the exact moment the opening appears — "I don't want to seem greedy," "the timing isn't quite right," "let's not rock the boat." Identify yours in advance, write it down, and the next time you feel it rising in your throat, silently name it as the excuse rather than obeying it: "this is the timing excuse, not new information." A pre-identified excuse loses a significant portion of its power the moment it's recognized as a repeat performance rather than a fresh, situation-specific concern.

Rehearse the version where you succeed, not just the version where you get through it. Most rehearsal focuses entirely on delivering the pitch and surviving the reaction. Spend real time — a few minutes, out loud — imagining the ask succeeding cleanly, the raise granted, the new prices holding, and specifically notice what feels uncomfortable about that imagined success. That discomfort is the actual target. You are far more likely to sabotage an outcome you haven't let yourself fully imagine wanting.

For asks that stretch across months rather than resolving in one conversation, set a hard cap on clarifying questions before you have to answer. The illustrator's eleven-month stall survived precisely because each additional question felt like reasonable diligence rather than avoidance. If you notice a decision extending past a second or third round of "just one more thing to check," give yourself a firm deadline — a specific date, chosen in advance — by which you commit to answering, using whatever information you have by then. Diligence has diminishing returns; past a certain point, additional questions are not making the decision better informed, they're making the deadline further away.

Both the physical therapist's employee and the restaurant owner eventually did make their moves, months later than they'd originally planned, once the pattern had a name. Her raise, when she finally asked for it directly instead of retreating at the last sentence, was approved within the same meeting, with an ease that made the months of stalling feel almost absurd in retrospect — not because the ask was ever going to be hard, but because the hardest part had never actually been her manager's response. It had been her own willingness to let the sentence land. The restaurant owner's new menu, when it finally launched, produced exactly one complaint in its first month, from a regular who grumbled about the price of a sandwich and ordered it anyway. The slow Tuesday he'd been protecting himself against never really materialized. What both of them discovered, in the end, wasn't that the ask was easy. It was that the version of the ask they'd been avoiding for years was considerably smaller, in reality, than the version they'd been rehearsing in their heads.

The illustrator, roughly eighteen months after losing the book cover project, is approached by the same publisher again with a second, comparable opportunity — evidently the working relationship had survived the earlier stall better than she'd feared. This time she gives herself one week, total, for questions, states that limit to the publisher up front, and answers within it. The project closes on schedule. She'll tell you now, with the benefit of hindsight on both outcomes side by side, that the eleven months of "diligence" the first time never actually produced better information than the one week did the second time. It only produced eleven more months of not having to say yes.

The ask you keep almost making was never really about the money on the other side of it — it was about the identity waiting for you the moment you said the number out loud. Say it anyway, and find out the identity fits.

Chapter 4 — The Generous Leak

Why Giving It Away Is the Hardest Version of This to Catch

The wire transfer takes four minutes to set up and she doesn't hesitate once during any of them.

Her freelance design business just closed the largest single contract of its six-year existence — a number that, after taxes, still represents more money arriving at once than she's ever held. She feels the number land the way you'd feel a wave land, and for about a day, she lets herself feel good about it. On the second day, her younger brother calls. He's behind on rent again, not for the first time, and there's a version of this call she's had a dozen times before where she offers fifty or a hundred dollars and feels the appropriate mixture of guilt and relief. This time is different. This time she offers to cover it — not one month, but three, plus what he owes on a credit card he mentions almost in passing. By the time she hangs up, she's transferred an amount that erases nearly the entire signing bonus. She feels, in the moment, generous, capable, like someone finally in a position to help. She does not feel, and would strongly resist the suggestion, that she just spent four minutes efficiently returning her balance to where it sat before the contract closed.

Nobody in her life would call this a problem. That's precisely what makes it the hardest version of the ceiling to catch — every other chapter in this book involves a choice that at least raises an eyebrow from an outside observer. A hasty car purchase. A stalled negotiation. Generosity toward a struggling family member raises no eyebrows at all. It's celebrated. It's the kind of story people tell at dinner as evidence of good character. Which means the release valve in this chapter is the one most protected from scrutiny, including your own — because who wants to examine, closely, whether their kindness was actually kind, or whether it was a getaway car.

A tech founder in his forties runs a version of this pattern at a scale two orders of magnitude larger, after an acquisition offer finally closes on a company he's built for nine years. In the weeks that follow, he becomes uncharacteristically, almost compulsively generous — grand tips left with a flourish in front of colleagues, an unsolicited and unnecessarily large investment in a friend's shaky startup, a habit of picking up every dinner check before anyone else can reach for it, every single time, regardless of who's at the table. Friends notice, and what they notice is generosity, and they say so, warmly, and he basks in it a little, because it does feel good. What none of them notice, because it isn't visible from any single instance, is the total: across eight weeks, a meaningful fraction of the acquisition proceeds has moved outward, through gestures that were each, individually, completely reasonable and kind, toward a running total that has quietly stopped looking like the number that made him so uneasy the day the deal closed.

A nurse practitioner in her fifties, newly promoted into a supervisory role with a substantial raise attached, offers a version of this pattern aimed inward at her own household rather than outward at friends or siblings. Within a month of the raise taking effect, she's quietly absorbed her adult daughter's car payment, started covering her elderly mother's grocery bill in full rather than the partial contribution she'd made for years, and picked up a new, larger monthly transfer to a nephew in college that nobody in the family actually asked her to increase. Each decision, examined alone, looks like a mother and daughter and aunt simply doing better by the people she loves now that she can. Examined together, the new obligations she's taken on total almost exactly the raise's monthly value, which means her own take-home pay, the thing the promotion was supposed to change, remains, in practice, identical to what it was before. She'll describe this, if asked, as being fortunate enough to finally help her family properly. She won't describe it, because she hasn't noticed it, as a raise that never once touched her own account.

What's actually happening

The core mechanism here is the same thermostat running throughout this book, but the specific psychological gearing that makes generosity such an effective and invisible release valve deserves its own name, and the clearest one comes from Leon Festinger's work on cognitive dissonance. Festinger's foundational research, dating to the 1950s, established that people experience genuine psychological discomfort when they hold two conflicting cognitions at once — in this case, "I am someone who doesn't have this much money" and "I currently have this much money" — and that the discomfort motivates a resolution, often through action rather than through simply updating the belief. Festinger's own experiments found something specifically relevant here: people will frequently resolve dissonance not by changing the belief that's easier to change, but by taking an action that restores consistency, even at real personal cost, because the action resolves the discomfort faster and more completely than the slower work of belief revision.

Generosity is, among the available dissonance-resolving actions, uniquely well suited to the job, for a reason worth naming precisely: it reduces the number while simultaneously reinforcing a self-concept that feels good rather than bad. The alarm purchase in Chapter 2 reduces the number but produces some ambient guilt alongside it — a nagging awareness of impulsiveness that at least leaves a faint trail. Generosity reduces the number and produces pride. It's a release valve with no exhaust smell. The designer isn't just resolving the discomfort of an unfamiliar balance; she's resolving it while reinforcing a story she likes — "I take care of my family," "I'm generous now that I can be" — which makes the transfer feel, from the inside, like growth rather than retreat. That's precisely what makes it so hard to interrupt. Every other chapter's pattern involves a moment of at least private unease. This one can feel, in the moment of doing it, like becoming a better person.

It's worth being precise about what this chapter is not arguing, because the line matters and it's easy to blur. This isn't a claim that generosity itself is suspect, or that helping family is something to be second-guessed on principle — that would replace one unhealthy relationship with money with another, trading a ceiling reflex for a withholding one, which is no improvement at all. Plenty of people give generously at financial high points for the simplest possible reason: they finally can, and they want to, and the amount is proportionate to both the need and their own new capacity. The distinguishing feature isn't the act of giving. It's the specific combination of speed, disproportion, and suspiciously exact timing — a transfer that lands within days of the windfall, sized with unusual precision to erase most or all of it, decided in minutes rather than the kind of longer deliberation most people apply to a gift of that scale. That combination is the signature. An isolated instance of fast generosity proves nothing on its own. It's the recurrence of that specific signature, across multiple windfalls, that turns a kind impulse into a legible pattern.

There is a further dynamic worth naming, drawn from research on what's sometimes called moral licensing — studies, including work by Nina Mazar and Chen-Bo Zhong among others, showing that a genuinely good or virtuous act can paradoxically license subsequent behavior a person wouldn't otherwise permit themselves, because the good act has "banked" a kind of moral credit. Applied here, the mechanism runs in a slightly different but related direction: the discomfort of an elevated financial identity gets resolved specifically through an act coded as moral, which does double duty — it lowers the number, and it also, in the same motion, provides a socially sanctioned, morally unimpeachable cover story for why the number came down, one that requires no further examination from anyone, including the person who gave the money away. Nobody asks a generous person to justify their generosity. That's exactly why the mechanism prefers this door over every other one available.

The nurse practitioner's version is worth returning to here, because it illustrates a variant this chapter hasn't fully named yet: generosity that flows not outward toward a single dramatic gesture, but sideways, distributed across several ongoing obligations that each individually look like reasonable family support. Her pattern is harder to catch than the designer's four-minute wire transfer precisely because it never happens in one visible moment — there's no single decision a person could point to and ask "was that really necessary?" Instead, the correction accumulates across three separate, smaller decisions, each made on a different day, none of which she experienced as connected to the others or to the raise. This is the moral-licensing mechanism operating in slow motion rather than all at once: each individual act of family support licenses the next, and by the time all three have compounded, the raise has been fully absorbed without a single moment that would have prompted her to notice the pattern, because there was never a single moment at all — only a month's worth of ordinary-looking kindness that happened, in aggregate, to add up with suspicious precision.

How to tell the difference. The clearest test here is arithmetic rather than intuition, precisely because intuition is the thing this chapter's mechanism is best at fooling. Total up, honestly, everything given away, loaned, or newly committed to in the four to six weeks following a financial high point, and compare that total to the size of the high point itself. Ordinary, healthy generosity rarely lands with mathematical precision — it's proportionate but rarely erases the gain entirely. The signature this chapter describes shows up specifically when the total, once you actually add it up, comes close enough to the full value of the windfall that the coincidence stops being plausible. Nobody sits down and calculates this in the moment. That's exactly why doing the arithmetic afterward, even once, tends to be so revealing.

What it costs you

The dollar cost, this time, tends to be larger than in the other chapters, precisely because it faces so little internal resistance — nobody's internal alarm bells go off during an act of generosity the way they might during an impulsive purchase, so there's no natural brake slowing the amount down. The designer's three-month rent-plus-credit-card transfer would likely have felt excessive to her if framed as "an impulsive gift," but framed as "helping my brother," it sailed through without a single moment of the hesitation that a car purchase of the same size would have triggered.

The relational cost is subtler and, over time, can be more corrosive than the dollar figure. Money given as an unconscious release valve rather than a considered choice tends to come with strings the giver doesn't fully realize are attached — a quiet expectation of gratitude proportional to the sacrifice it didn't actually feel like at the time, a resentment that can surface months later when the giver's own finances feel tight again and the "generosity" starts to look, in retrospect, like it was never fully theirs to give so freely. The recipient, meanwhile, often senses something is slightly off about the transaction without being able to name it — a gift given from discomfort rather than surplus can carry an odd charge, a neediness underneath the generosity, that a gift given from genuine, considered abundance does not.

And underneath both of those sits the same cost that runs through every chapter in this book: the actual goal the money could have funded — the retirement account, the business runway, the next stage of growth — never gets to benefit from the milestone that was supposed to fund it, because the milestone got quietly redirected before it could compound into anything. The founder's nine years of building produced a number that, eight weeks later, looks a great deal like the number he had before, except now dispersed across a dozen acts of generosity he'll remember fondly and none of which moved him meaningfully closer to whatever he actually said he wanted the acquisition money for.

There is one more cost worth naming, quieter than the others and specific to this chapter: the loss of ever finding out what the designer or the founder would have actually chosen to do with the money, given time and a clear head, rather than an urgent need to make the discomfort of a new number go away. The brother's rent may well have been worth covering. The friend's startup may well have been worth backing. But those decisions, made in the fog of a four-minute wire transfer or an eight-week generosity spree, were never really evaluated on their own merits — they were selected because they were available, plausible, and fast, not because they were the best use of the money among the many uses it might have had. Real generosity, chosen deliberately, and reflexive generosity, discharged automatically, can look identical from the outside and cost the giver in completely different ways. Only one of them actually reflects what the giver would have wanted, examined calmly, a month later.

The overrides

Separate the impulse from the amount before you act on either. The desire to help someone you love after a financial win is very often completely legitimate and worth honoring — this override isn't asking you to become withholding. It's asking you to decouple two decisions that arrive fused: whether to help, and how much. Decide the first quickly if you want to. Decide the second only after a deliberate pause, ideally using a number you'd have considered appropriate a month before the windfall, not a number calibrated by how uncomfortable the new balance currently feels.

Ask yourself the uncomfortable diagnostic question directly. Before a large generous gesture that arrives within weeks of a financial high point, ask: "Would I be giving this much if my balance had stayed exactly where it was a month ago?" You don't have to answer out loud, and you don't have to let the answer stop you. But asking the question honestly, every time, breaks the automatic quality that makes this pattern so hard to catch. A release valve that requires a conscious checkpoint before it fires isn't a reflex anymore. It's a decision.

The Move: fund the generosity from a separate, pre-decided pool, not from the fresh windfall directly. Before any major financial milestone arrives — and you can do this in advance, the moment you see one approaching — decide on a fixed, modest giving amount as a matter of policy, completely separate from whatever amount a future emotional moment might otherwise produce. When the urge to be generous arrives at the high point, as it likely will, draw only from that pre-decided pool. This does two things at once: it lets real generosity happen, uncorrupted by the reflex, and it makes the reflex's favorite door much harder to walk through unnoticed, because the pool has a bottom and the bottom is visible.

Give yourself permission to help in a form that doesn't touch the windfall at all. If the underlying urge is genuinely about wanting to support someone you love rather than about discharging discomfort, notice that money is not the only available form that support can take — time, connections, advice, practical help with a job search or a budget, none of which run through the same account the ceiling reflex is trying to correct. Separating the desire to help from the specific mechanism of a large cash transfer often reveals which one you were actually after.

Let the gift be smaller and still count. If you notice the urge to give in a way that specifically erases the milestone — not help that's proportionate, but help that's suspiciously exactly enough to bring the number back down — give a genuinely meaningful but smaller amount instead, and sit with the discomfort of not having "solved" the other person's problem completely. A smaller gift that leaves your own gains intact is not a lesser act of love. It's evidence that the love and the ceiling reflex have finally been pulled apart from each other.

Audit standing obligations after a raise before adding new ones. For anyone whose version of this pattern looks like the nurse practitioner's — a raise quietly absorbed into a cluster of existing family support commitments rather than one dramatic gesture — the useful discipline is a deliberate pause before increasing any recurring support in the weeks immediately following a raise. Write down what you were already contributing before the raise, and treat any increase as its own separate decision, made consciously and on its own timeline, rather than something that happens automatically the moment new capacity appears. Ongoing support that grows in step with your income isn't wrong. Support that grows precisely enough to cancel a raise out, every single time, without ever being consciously decided, is the pattern worth catching.

The designer, a year after the six-figure contract, hits a comparable milestone again — a second large client win, close in size to the first. Her brother calls again, a different crisis this time, equally real. She feels the same immediate pull to solve it completely, the same four-minute urgency. This time, she pauses, asks herself the diagnostic question, and notices that the honest answer is no — she would not, a month ago, have offered to cover three months of anything. She offers a smaller amount instead, genuinely useful, sized the way she'd have sized it in any ordinary month, and directs the rest of the milestone toward the retirement contribution she'd actually planned for it. Her brother is still helped. Her own progress, this time, stays intact. Nothing about her capacity for generosity changed between the two calls. What changed was that the second time, she had a question to ask before her hand reached for the transfer button.

The nurse practitioner, at her next annual review, receives a second raise, smaller than the first but still meaningful. This time, before the month even starts, she sits down and writes out exactly what she's currently contributing to her daughter, her mother, and her nephew — real numbers, on paper, for the first time in years. When the familiar pull arrives to quietly increase all three the moment the new number lands, she notices it arriving, checks it against the list, and makes one conscious decision instead of three unconscious ones: a modest, deliberate increase to her mother's support alone, sized specifically and chosen on purpose, with the rest of the raise going, for the first time in her career, into an account with her own name on it.

Generosity was never the problem here. Timing was the evidence, and evidence doesn't lie the way a good story can. Give because you want to give, on a schedule and at a scale you'd choose in any ordinary month — not because a number just got uncomfortable and needed somewhere plausible to go.

Chapter 5 — The Bet That Wasn't Like You

Why Success Makes You Suddenly, Uncharacteristically Reckless

Six weeks after his consulting firm lands its first six-figure retainer client — the deal he'd spent two years positioning for — he puts a third of the firm's operating cushion into a cryptocurrency position he heard about from a guy at a conference, based on research that amounts to one enthusiastic conversation and a chart that looked like it was going up.

This is a man who built spreadsheets to model three different pricing scenarios before setting his hourly rate. Who has an actual, written investment policy for the firm's retained earnings, drafted with an advisor, reviewed annually. Who would, if you'd described this exact trade to him eight weeks earlier — a third of the cushion, one conversation's worth of research, no stop-loss, no position sizing discipline — have called it reckless without hesitation, maybe even used it as a cautionary example with a client. He makes the trade on a Tuesday afternoon, between calls, in about eleven minutes. The position craters within three weeks. He tells his business partner it was "a calculated risk that didn't pay off," which is not really a lie, exactly, but isn't the truth either — there was no calculation. There was a number that had just gotten larger than it had ever been, and a bet that, whether he could have named it this way or not, had exactly the effect of making it smaller again.

A retail worker several income tiers below him runs an almost identical program at a scale that makes it easier, from the outside, to see clearly. She's just paid off the last of a debt that's followed her for nine years — a genuine, hard-won milestone, tracked on a spreadsheet she updates every payday, celebrated with actual tears the night the final payment cleared. Three weeks later, with the first paycheck that isn't earmarked for debt in almost a decade, she puts nearly all of it into a single stock a coworker mentioned, on a tip with no research behind it beyond "it's supposed to go up," in an amount that would have seemed unthinkable to her a month earlier, when every dollar had a job and none of them were "supposed to go up." The stock drops. The money that was, for the first time in years, actually hers to build with is gone within a month, and the debt-free number she cried over starts, within two pay cycles, to look a great deal like the debt-carrying number she just spent nine years escaping.

A veterinarian in his late thirties, newly made partner at the practice where he's worked for a decade, offers a version of this pattern that shows up not in a market or a casino but at a card table among friends. He's never been a serious gambler — a friendly poker night once a month, stakes low enough that losing a hand barely registers. Two weeks after the partnership is finalized, at the same monthly game with the same friends, he starts playing differently: bigger bets, looser calls, a willingness to chase a hand that the version of him from two months earlier would have folded without a second thought. His friends notice and rib him about it, good-naturedly, assuming the new partnership has made him feel flush. He loses, across that single night, an amount that would have seemed absurd to risk at that table a month earlier — not enough to be a financial catastrophe, but enough that he has to quietly explain a withdrawal to his wife the following week, in a conversation that makes him uncomfortable in a way he can't quite locate. He'll tell you he just got unlucky with the cards. He won't tell you, because he hasn't noticed it, that the recklessness started exactly at the moment his professional identity changed, and ended, just as precisely, once the loss had brought his sense of himself back down to a size that felt, underneath the discomfort, oddly familiar.

What's actually happening

The behavior in this chapter looks, on the surface, like ordinary bad luck with an investment — the kind of story that happens to plenty of people who have nothing to do with a ceiling reflex at all. What separates an ordinary bad bet from a ceiling-driven one is the same diagnostic this whole book keeps returning to: the timing, and the mismatch with the person's usual behavior. A person who takes speculative risks regularly, as a matter of general temperament, making one that doesn't pay off is just an unlucky outcome from an ordinary process. A person who is otherwise careful, disciplined, and risk-averse, making one wildly out-of-character bet within weeks of a financial high point, is showing you something different — a process interruption, not an ordinary outcome.

Daniel Kahneman and Amos Tversky's prospect theory, foundational to modern behavioral economics, offers the clearest lens available for what's happening underneath. Their research demonstrated that people don't evaluate outcomes against some fixed, objective standard — they evaluate them relative to a reference point, and their appetite for risk shifts dramatically depending on whether they perceive themselves as currently ahead of that reference point or behind it. One of the more striking findings to emerge from this tradition, sometimes called the "house money effect" after later work extending prospect theory into gambling contexts, is that people become measurably more willing to take large risks with money they perceive as recent, unearned-feeling gains than with money they perceive as their baseline capital — treating a windfall less like "my money" and more like the casino's money, temporarily in their possession, which can be gambled with a recklessness that would never be extended to funds that feel like they were always, solidly, theirs.

The veterinarian's poker night is worth pausing on specifically, because it isolates the mechanism from money entirely and shows it operating on identity alone. The stakes at his monthly game are, by his own household's standards, trivial — losing badly for one night wouldn't meaningfully dent his finances the way the consultant's cryptocurrency position or the retail worker's stock tip could. What changed wasn't his relationship to a large sum of money. It was his relationship to a new professional identity, arriving two weeks earlier, that his nervous system hadn't yet integrated. The recklessness at the card table wasn't really about the cards, any more than the alarm purchase in Chapter 2 was really about a car. It was the fastest available discharge for a discomfort that had nothing to do with poker and everything to do with the word "partner" now attached to his name — proof that this mechanism doesn't require large dollar amounts to fire. It only requires an identity that recently, suddenly, changed size.

It's worth noting what makes this chapter's version of the ceiling especially dangerous relative to the others in this book: variance. A stalled ask costs you the difference between two numbers, bounded and knowable. An alarm purchase costs you the price of whatever you bought, also bounded. A reckless bet has no such ceiling on its own downside — the consultant could have lost nothing, or he could have lost the entire third of the cushion and then some if the position had involved leverage, which many speculative positions do. The ceiling reflex doesn't care about the size of the correction it produces. It only cares that the number moves back toward familiar territory, and a genuinely reckless bet is one of the few available mechanisms in this book capable of overshooting that target by a wide margin, turning a modest correction into a genuine financial setback that outlives the original discomfort by years.

This explains part of what's happening in both scenes, but not all of it, because neither the consultant nor the retail worker consciously experienced the money as a windfall in the "found money" sense — both had worked hard and directly for what they now had. The deeper layer, specific to the ceiling mechanism, is that the reference point itself had just shifted upward, and the discomfort of the new, higher reference point creates its own appetite for a bet that could resolve the discomfort quickly, in either direction. A win at the new number would, paradoxically, be almost as threatening as a loss — it would only push the reference point further from where it felt correct. A loss, on the other hand, does something the ceiling reflex actually wants: it returns the number to a range that feels psychologically survivable. This is speculative in a way self-verification and prospect theory alone don't fully cover, but it fits a pattern researchers studying self-handicapping — including foundational work by Edward Jones and Steven Berglas in the 1970s — have long documented in other domains: people will sometimes create obstacles to their own success, consciously or not, specifically because success itself, and the raised expectations that come with it, feels more threatening to manage than a return to a familiar, lower baseline.

How to tell the difference. Not every investment loss following a windfall is this mechanism at work — markets are genuinely volatile, and a well-researched position can lose money for reasons that have nothing to do with a ceiling reflex. The distinguishing feature is process, not outcome. A genuine investment decision, even a losing one, typically follows the same diligence a person applies to their other financial decisions — comparable research depth, comparable position sizing, comparable time spent deciding. The ceiling-driven bet breaks from the person's own established process specifically, and specifically around a financial high point: less research than usual, larger size than usual, faster decision than usual, all three at once. A single one of those departures might just be an off day. All three together, arriving within weeks of a windfall, is the pattern this chapter describes.

What it costs you

The dollar cost here tends to run larger than in most of this book's other chapters, because reckless bets, by definition, carry more variance than a purchase or a loan — the downside isn't capped the way a car payment is capped. The consultant didn't just spend a third of the firm's cushion. He put it somewhere with genuine potential for near-total loss, and got close to it. The retail worker didn't just give money away. She converted nine years of disciplined debt repayment into a single month's speculative loss, a trade so lopsided in time that it's hard to look at directly.

The subtler cost is what a single reckless bet does to a person's trust in their own judgment going forward, particularly because — unlike the alarm purchase or the stalled ask — this pattern often gets misfiled as an isolated lapse rather than recognized as a pattern at all. "I made one bad call" is a story a careful person can tell themselves once, plausibly, and move on from without ever examining the timing. It's only when you look across several financial high points — the promotion, the debt payoff, the client win, the equity vest — and notice that an out-of-character risky bet shows up in the weeks after most of them, that the pattern stops being a bad-luck story and becomes a legible mechanism. Most people never do that accounting, which means the pattern gets to repeat, indefinitely, each instance re-filed as a fresh, unrelated coincidence.

There's a specific relational cost worth naming for anyone in a shared financial life, because the consultant's story doesn't end with the trade — it continues into a conversation with his business partner that never quite tells the whole truth. Partners, spouses, and co-founders who witness a single uncharacteristic reckless bet are often willing to extend real grace, because it does genuinely happen to careful people once in a while. What erodes trust over time isn't the loss itself. It's the pattern of explaining each instance as isolated, which a partner eventually starts to notice doesn't hold up, and which introduces a specific, hard-to-name doubt into the relationship: not "can I trust this person with money," exactly, but "can I trust this person's account of their own decisions," which is a harder doubt to resolve, because it isn't about competence. It's about whether the story you're being told matches what's actually happening.

There's a cost specific to the veterinarian's version worth naming too, small in dollar terms but instructive precisely because of its smallness: the discomfort of the uncomfortable conversation with his wife the following week didn't resolve anything either. He explained the withdrawal, she accepted the explanation, and the underlying mechanism went right on operating, unexamined, ready to fire again at the next identity threshold he crosses — a second partnership, an expanded role, whatever comes next. Small-stakes instances of this pattern are easy to dismiss precisely because the dollar cost doesn't force a reckoning the way a larger loss might. That makes them, in a strange way, more dangerous over a long career than a single large loss would be, because they never accumulate enough visible damage to prompt the kind of scrutiny that might actually catch the pattern before it repeats at a much larger scale, on a much larger identity threshold, somewhere down the road.

The overrides

Build a bright line before you're near it, not during. Decide, now, while no windfall is active and no discomfort is pulling at you, on a hard rule for what percentage of any new gain you're willing to put into a speculative position without a formal research and sizing process behind it. Write the number down somewhere you'll actually see it again. The rule needs to exist before the pull arrives, because the pull itself is specifically designed to feel like an exception the rule doesn't apply to.

Apply your own normal process, on purpose, as a test. The next time you feel drawn toward an investment decision that arrives fast, on thin research, close to a financial high point, deliberately run it through whatever process you'd apply to any other investment decision — the spreadsheet, the advisor conversation, the waiting period. If the opportunity can't survive your own normal diligence, that's not bad luck robbing you of a good trade. That's the diligence doing exactly what it's for. Most reckless-bet regret isn't regret about the loss — it's regret about skipping a process the person already knew, and would have used on any ordinary Tuesday.

The Move: when you notice yourself about to break your own usual pattern, say the mismatch out loud before you act. Literally say the sentence: "I don't normally make decisions this fast, with this little research, at this size — and I'm about to, right after [the raise / the payoff / the deal]." You don't have to stop yourself after saying it. Just say it, out loud or in writing, before you click confirm. Naming the mismatch in real time, rather than explaining it away afterward, is often enough on its own to break the automatic quality that lets the bet slide through unexamined.

Involve a second person in any decision that meets three specific conditions. If a financial decision arrives fast, is sized larger than your normal position sizing or spending pattern, and follows within a month of a genuine financial high point, make it a hard rule that you run the decision past one other person before acting — a partner, a business partner, an advisor, anyone whose presence alone tends to slow down impulsive action. The rule doesn't need to apply to every decision, which would be exhausting and unnecessary. It needs to apply specifically to decisions that meet all three conditions at once, because that specific combination is this chapter's signature, and a second set of eyes is one of the most reliable circuit breakers available for a pattern that thrives on being executed alone, fast, and unexamined.

Route the discomfort of the new number somewhere other than a bet. If what's actually driving the urge is the raw discomfort of an unfamiliar financial position — which it usually is, whether or not the bet gets dressed up in the language of opportunity — address that discomfort directly, the way Chapter 2's override suggests: sit with it, name it, let it be uncomfortable without acting on it. A reckless bet is one of the fastest routes back to a familiar number. It is not the only route, and it's worth having a slower, less expensive one ready before the urge arrives.

Notice when the stakes are trivial but the mismatch is still present, and treat it as data anyway. The veterinarian's poker losses were never going to bankrupt his household, which is exactly why the pattern was easy to dismiss as ordinary bad luck at cards. Low-stakes instances of out-of-character recklessness are worth taking just as seriously as high-stakes ones, not because of what they cost, but because of what they reveal about the mechanism's presence and timing. A small, cheap version of the pattern caught early is a far better teacher than a large, expensive version caught only after it's already done real damage.

The retail worker, roughly a year after her debt-free milestone and the speculative trade that undid most of it, reaches a second, larger milestone — six months of consistent saving, the first real cushion she's ever held. She notices the itch arrive on schedule, almost exactly the way it did the first time, a coworker mentioning another hot tip, the same compressed urgency to act fast on thin information. This time she recognizes the itch by name, waits, and runs the opportunity — genuinely, seriously — through the kind of research she'd apply to anything else, which the tip does not survive. She doesn't make the trade. The cushion stays intact. She describes the moment afterward not as a triumph of willpower, exactly, but as something closer to recognition: she'd seen this specific itch before, knew where it led, and simply declined to follow it a second time. That's a smaller, less dramatic story than the first one. It's also the entire mechanism of change this book is built around, working exactly as intended.

The veterinarian, roughly a year after the poker night, is offered a second, larger ownership stake in a satellite location the practice is opening. He notices, this time, a familiar restlessness arrive in the days after signing — an urge to do something uncharacteristic, though nothing specific has presented itself yet. Rather than wait for the urge to find its outlet, he tells his wife directly what he's noticing, names the poker night as the pattern he's watching for, and asks her to flag it if she sees anything resembling it. Nothing dramatic happens at that month's game. He plays exactly as he always has, stakes unchanged, decisions unchanged. The identity shift settled without needing a card table to discharge it into, because this time, the discomfort had somewhere else to go: a named pattern, and a witness.

The bet that didn't sound like you probably wasn't about the opportunity at all — it was the fastest plausible route back to a number that felt survivable. Recognize the mismatch before you place it, not after you're explaining the loss.

Chapter 6 — The Deal You Talked Yourself Out Of

Why Success Sometimes Gets Sabotaged Before It Can Fully Land

The email sits in his drafts folder for six days, finished, ready to send, a single line of easy small talk away from closing the largest contract of his career.

He runs a small architectural firm, four employees, a decade of slow, real growth behind him. The client on the other end of this email is a developer with three more projects in the pipeline after this one — the kind of relationship that, if it lands well, doesn't just fund this year, it changes the trajectory of the whole firm for the next five. Every term is agreed. The client is, by every signal available, ready. All that's left is a reply confirming a start date that was, itself, the client's own suggestion. He opens the draft on day one, day three, day five. On day six, instead of sending it, he adds a clause to the contract that wasn't part of any of the negotiated terms — a scope adjustment nobody asked for, framed as "just protecting both of us," that changes the payment structure in a way no reasonable developer would accept without another full round of negotiation. The client's response, when it comes, is polite, confused, and cooler than every previous exchange. The deal doesn't die outright. It just slows, stalls, and eventually gets quietly absorbed by a competitor who didn't reopen anything.

He will tell his employees, and eventually believe it himself, that he was "just being careful," that the clause was reasonable due diligence, that the client "wasn't serious enough" if a fair protection clause could derail things. None of that survives close inspection. The clause wasn't in the term sheet either side had spent six weeks negotiating. It appeared, specifically, on day six of a stall that had nothing to do with contract terms and everything to do with what it would mean, concretely and irreversibly, to become the kind of firm that lands deals like this one.

A therapist in private practice, a decade into a modest solo practice with a loyal but limited client base, gets approached by a group practice with an offer to bring her on as a partner — not an employee, a genuine partner, with a caseload and compensation structure that would roughly double her income and put her name on a much larger, much more visible platform. She says yes in the meeting, enthusiastically, and means it. Over the following two weeks, in the process of finalizing details, she becomes almost impossible to schedule with — canceling calls, taking days to answer emails she'd normally answer within hours, raising a series of small logistical concerns that, individually, sound reasonable and, in aggregate, read as someone quietly trying to make the deal difficult enough that someone else calls it off first. The group practice, patient at first, eventually moves forward with a different candidate. She tells herself, and her closest friend, that "it probably wasn't the right fit anyway" — a sentence that arrives suspiciously fast for a decision that, three weeks earlier, she'd described as the best professional opportunity of her career.

A landscaping business owner in his forties offers a third variation, this one sabotaged not through a clause or a delay but through price. He's approached by a property management company that oversees a dozen commercial sites, offering him an exclusive, multi-year contract that would roughly quadruple his annual revenue and require him to finally hire the crew he's talked about hiring for years. Everything about the negotiation goes smoothly until it's his turn to name the number — a bid he's had weeks to prepare, based on real cost calculations he trusts. In the meeting, without planning to, he quotes a figure nearly thirty percent below what his own spreadsheet says the contract is worth, a number so favorable to the property management company that their representative visibly hesitates, almost suspicious of the gap, before accepting on the spot. He drives home elated, and it's only that night, running the numbers again out of habit, that he realizes what he did — not underbid by a rounding error, but underbid by an amount too large to be an honest mistake, in the exact meeting where accepting the real number would have meant becoming, overnight, the owner of a company large enough to need employees, payroll, and a scale of responsibility he'd never actually operated at before.

What's actually happening

This is the chapter where the ceiling's fingerprints are hardest to see, because unlike an alarm purchase or a reckless bet, the self-sabotage here doesn't touch money directly at all. It touches the deal, the opportunity, the relationship that would have produced the money — intercepting the reflex one full step earlier in the chain, so early that it can hide behind entirely plausible business language. A protective clause. A scheduling concern. A fit that "didn't feel right." Every individual move is defensible. The pattern only becomes visible in the aggregate, and specifically in the timing: the sabotaging behavior arrives not randomly across the negotiation, but clustered right at the point the deal has become real enough to actually change the person's financial and professional identity.

Albert Bandura's research on self-efficacy — a person's belief in their own capacity to execute at a given level — offers the clearest lens for what's happening here. Bandura's decades of work established that self-efficacy beliefs aren't just a byproduct of a person's actual capability; they actively shape behavior, often becoming self-fulfilling, because people tend to act in ways consistent with what they believe themselves capable of sustaining, independent of what they're actually capable of. A person whose self-efficacy has been calibrated, over years, around running "a small, steady, four-person firm" or "a modest, loyal solo practice" doesn't just doubt their capacity for the next tier up in some abstract sense. They unconsciously act in ways that keep them at the tier their self-efficacy beliefs already validate, because operating above that tier requires sustaining a level of performance and visibility their internal model doesn't yet certify as theirs to hold. The clause, the stalled scheduling — these aren't sabotage in the sense of a person trying to fail. They're closer to a system quietly declining a role it doesn't yet believe it can sustain, and finding a face-saving exit before that mismatch has to be discovered in public, in front of the new client or the new partners, rather than privately, in a drafts folder no one else will ever see.

It's worth distinguishing this chapter's mechanism carefully from Chapter 3's stalled ask, because on the surface they can look similar — both involve a person pulling back right as a financial opportunity nears completion. The difference is in what's being protected. The stalled ask protects against ever having to cross the threshold at all; the person simply never sends the message, never has the conversation, and the number never gets the chance to change. The sabotaged deal is stranger and, in some ways, more revealing, because the person has already said yes. They've already crossed the threshold verbally, already accepted the identity shift in principle. The sabotage happens anyway, after the yes, specifically because saying yes and actually inhabiting the yes turn out to be two different psychological events, and it's the second one — the actual arrival, the actual becoming — that the reflex is defending against. This is why the sabotage so often looks like second-guessing rather than outright refusal: the person isn't undoing a decision they never wanted. They're undoing a decision they did want, the moment it stopped being hypothetical.

There's a second mechanism compounding this one, worth naming because it explains the specific *timing* — why the sabotage clusters so tightly around the moment the deal becomes real rather than showing up earlier, when it might have been easier to simply decline. Research on the fear of success — a less famous cousin of fear of failure, studied initially by Matina Horner in the 1960s and refined by subsequent researchers — documented that some people experience anticipated success itself as threatening, specifically because of what success is expected to cost: increased visibility, higher expectations, a changed relationship to peers who haven't kept pace, the loss of a familiar identity built around modesty or struggle. The architect isn't afraid the deal will fail. He's afraid, at some level he wouldn't put in these words, of what it means to become someone whose firm closes deals like this — the pressure of the next three projects the client mentioned, the employees he'd need to hire, the version of himself required to sustain a firm at that scale rather than the one he's spent ten years learning how to run. The sabotage arrives exactly when the deal stops being hypothetical and starts requiring him to actually become that person. Before that point, there was nothing yet to defend against. At that point, there suddenly is.

How to tell the difference. Legitimate last-minute concerns exist, and killing or restructuring a deal at the finish line is sometimes exactly the right call — new information can arrive late, and a genuinely bad deal deserves to fall apart no matter how far along it's gotten. What separates ordinary diligence from this chapter's pattern is whether the concern points outward or inward. A legitimate late concern usually points at the deal itself — a term that's genuinely unfavorable, a counterparty whose reliability is now in question, numbers that don't work the way they first appeared to. The ceiling-driven version points, even if the language used doesn't admit it, at the person's own capacity to sustain what comes next — vague unease about the workload, the visibility, the pace, dressed up in the language of a business concern because that's the only vocabulary available for it. If you can articulate the objection as a specific, falsifiable claim about the deal's terms, it's probably real. If the objection dissolves the moment you try to state it that specifically, it probably isn't about the deal at all.

What it costs you

The dollar cost of a sabotaged deal is often the largest single figure in this entire book, because unlike a purchase or a bet, a lost deal doesn't just cost what was spent — it costs the entire multi-year trajectory the deal would have opened. The architect didn't just lose one contract. He lost the three follow-on projects the client mentioned, and every referral that client's network would likely have produced, and the five years of compounding growth that came from just this one relationship landing instead of stalling. This is the chapter where the ceiling's arithmetic is most brutal, because the cost isn't a single transaction. It's an entire branch of the future that quietly closes, one clause and one canceled call at a time.

The harder cost to name is what happens to a person's read on their own career after enough of these accumulate. Because each sabotage event gets explained away individually — bad fit, bad timing, overcautious but reasonable — a person can go years without ever connecting the dots into a pattern, and instead develop a broader, more diffuse belief that opportunities like this "just don't work out" for them, or that they're "not the type" who gets the big break, when the accurate description is closer to: they were offered the big break, multiple times, and quietly declined to let it land, in ways specific and clustered enough to have a name.

There's a cost to the other party in the deal, too, worth naming because it's easy to think of this pattern as self-contained, affecting only the person doing the sabotaging. The developer on the other end of the architect's email spent real time, real trust, and real internal capital advocating for this partnership, likely against competing bids or competing priorities inside his own organization. The therapist's group practice spent weeks structuring a partnership offer specifically around her, turning away or delaying other candidates in the process. When a deal collapses at the finish line for reasons that don't hold up to scrutiny, it doesn't just cost the person doing the sabotaging. It quietly damages their reputation with exactly the people most positioned to bring them the next big opportunity, because from the outside, a pattern of promising engagement followed by late, unexplained friction reads as unreliability, not as an internal psychological struggle nobody else can see.

The landscaper's underbid carries a cost worth isolating on its own, because it shows this chapter's mechanism can technically "succeed" — the deal closes, nobody walks away, everyone shakes hands — while still fully accomplishing the ceiling's actual goal. He didn't lose the contract. He kept it, at a price roughly thirty percent below its real value, which means the multi-year relationship he was so afraid of fully inhabiting now exists, but permanently underfunded relative to what it should be paying him. Every year of that contract, every renewal, every additional site the property management company adds to the agreement, compounds off a number that was never actually correct. This is arguably a worse outcome than an outright lost deal, because a lost deal at least leaves the door open for a future, correctly priced opportunity with a different client. An accepted, underpriced deal locks the discount in for years, disguised as a win.

The overrides

Watch your own behavior specifically at the point a deal becomes real, not before. The sabotage in this chapter rarely shows up during initial negotiation, when the outcome is still hypothetical — it shows up right as terms firm up and a start date approaches. Build a habit of paying closer attention to your own responsiveness, mood, and behavior specifically in that narrow window, because that's where the reflex, if it's present, will actually surface.

Ask a trusted, uninvolved third party to review any last-minute change before you send it. If you notice yourself adding a new term, raising a new concern, or introducing friction into a deal that had, until recently, been moving smoothly, run the change past someone with no stake in the outcome before you act on it. Ask them plainly: "Does this look like a reasonable business adjustment, or does it look like I'm trying to make this harder than it needs to be?" An outside read, at the exact moment the internal read is least trustworthy, is one of the most reliable circuit breakers available for this specific pattern.

The Move: when you notice hesitation at the finish line of something you genuinely wanted, name what completing it would actually require of you, specifically. Not vaguely — specifically. Write down, in plain language, what your life and identity look like the week after this deal closes: the new scale, the new visibility, the new expectations. Most finish-line sabotage isn't really about the deal. It's about an unexamined fear of the identity on the other side of it, and unexamined fears are far more powerful than named ones. Naming it precisely —

"closing this means I become someone who runs a firm this size" — often does more to defuse the sabotage than any amount of willpower applied to simply forcing yourself to hit send.

Distinguish genuine new information from manufactured friction. Not every second thought after a yes is sabotage — sometimes real due diligence turns up a genuine problem, and killing a deal for a legitimate reason is a sound business decision, not a symptom. The test is origin: did the concern arrive from something external and new — a fact you didn't have before, a term that genuinely changed — or did it arrive from nowhere in particular, generated internally, right on schedule with the deal's approach to completion? Concerns with an external, traceable origin deserve full weight. Concerns that seem to have appeared out of the general anxiety of the moment deserve a slower, more skeptical look before you act on them.

Let someone else hold you to the yes you already gave. Once you've said yes to something significant, tell at least one person outside the deal itself — a partner, a mentor, a close colleague — that you've said yes, and specifically what it would look like if you started backing away from it. This doesn't remove your ability to change your mind for legitimate reasons. It removes your ability to quietly sabotage the yes without anyone, including yourself, noticing it's happening.

When the sabotage arrives as a favorable number instead of a delay, apply the same scrutiny you'd apply to any other last-minute change. The landscaper's underbid never looked like sabotage from the outside — it looked like a deal closing smoothly. Any number you find yourself naming in the room, on the spot, without reference to the figure you prepared in advance, deserves a pause before you let it stand, even if — especially if — the number in the moment feels easier to say out loud than the one you calculated beforehand. If a bid or a rate arrives from your mouth without matching the number on the page in front of you, treat that gap as information, not as spontaneity.

The architect, roughly a year later, is approached by a different, even larger client, and notices the familiar clause-drafting impulse arrive again, right on schedule, a few days before the contract was due to be finalized. This time, having named the pattern from the previous near-miss, he does something different: he calls his original developer client, the one from the deal that stalled a year earlier, and asks, directly, whether the confusing clause had actually been the reason things cooled. The developer, candidly, confirms it was. That single conversation does more to interrupt the pattern than any amount of private resolve could have, because it converts an abstract, theoretical cost into a concrete, confirmed one — proof, from an actual outside source, that the sabotage had real consequences the first time, which makes it considerably harder to talk himself into repeating it the second.

The therapist, still building her solo caseload two years after the declined partnership, gets a second inbound offer from a different group practice, smaller this time but structured similarly. She notices the familiar cancellation urge arrive within days of accepting — a scheduling conflict here, a logistical question there — and this time she does the override directly: she tells her closest colleague, out loud, exactly what she said yes to and exactly what backing away from it would look like if she started stalling. Having said it out loud to someone who will actually ask how it's going turns out to be enough. She keeps every scheduled call. The partnership closes on the original timeline. She'll tell you, if you ask, that nothing about the second opportunity felt easier than the first. What was different was that this time, she had a name for what almost happened before, and a person who'd notice if she let it happen again.

The landscaper, roughly a year after the underbid contract, is approached by a second property management company with a similarly large opportunity. In the meeting, when it comes time to name his number, he catches the familiar urge to shave the figure down before it leaves his mouth — and, having written the target number on an index card and kept it visibly on the table in front of him, simply reads it aloud instead. The client accepts without negotiating, exactly as the first client had, at a number this time that actually matches what his spreadsheet says the work is worth. He hires his first two employees within the year.

Look again at the clause, the schedule, the "fit" that suddenly felt wrong. None of that was ever the real

objection. The real objection was who you'd have to become to close it. Notice the fear before it turns into a clause, and send the email anyway.

Chapter 7 — The Discount You Keep Giving Yourself

Why the Old Price Follows You Long After You've Outgrown It

She's been freelancing for eleven years, and her rate has moved twice in that time — both increases initiated by clients who, embarrassed on her behalf, insisted on paying her more than she'd asked for.

Her actual output, by any external measure, has changed enormously over those eleven years. Her early work was competent. Her current work — informed by hundreds of projects, a reputation strong enough that new clients now arrive by referral rather than by pitching — routinely produces results her clients describe, unprompted, as worth several times what she charges. She knows this, intellectually. She has, more than once, drafted an email announcing a rate increase and gotten as far as a specific new number. Then she quietly lowered that number by twenty or thirty percent before sending it, "just to be safe." The result is an adjustment so modest it barely keeps pace with inflation, let alone her actual growth. She has done this three separate times across eleven years. Each time, she tells herself this is the year she'll revisit it properly. Each time, the number she eventually sends is close enough to her old number that clients barely notice a change at all.

A therapist newly out of a group practice and building a solo caseload for the first time runs a version of the identical pattern from the opposite direction — not an old rate she's failing to raise, but a new one she's failing to set correctly from the start. She researches market rates thoroughly, understands clearly that her training and specialization justify a fee at the higher end of her local range, and then, in the actual moment of publishing her rate sheet, sets a number closer to what she was paid as a junior associate three years earlier — a number that has nothing to do with her actual qualifications now and everything to do with the last number she remembers feeling was "hers." Within a year, she's fully booked, turning away clients weekly, charging a fee that a simple survey of comparable local practices would tell her is roughly forty percent below what the market would readily bear. She isn't underpriced because she doesn't know better. She's underpriced because a rate she outgrew years ago is still, somewhere below conscious calculation, the number that feels like it belongs to her.

A general contractor in his fifties, running a well-regarded renovation business for over twenty years, offers a third version worth naming because it shows how this pattern survives even overwhelming external proof. Every single competitor he's ever compared notes with at industry meetups charges noticeably more per square foot than he does, for comparable or lesser work. Clients regularly express open surprise at how reasonable his quotes are, sometimes even asking, uneasily, whether he's sure the number is right. He's seen this evidence, directly, for two decades. He still quotes from a rate card he built in his early thirties, adjusted only for material cost inflation, never once revisited for what his actual decades of accumulated skill and reputation are worth on the open market. Ask him why, and he'll tell you he doesn't want to price himself out of the neighborhood he grew up doing work in — a real, sympathetic concern, and also, on inspection, one that doesn't hold up, since the neighborhood in question has changed considerably in twenty years and most of his current clients aren't from it at all.

The rate card isn't protecting the neighborhood. It's protecting the number that felt right to a thirty-year-old who hadn't yet built the reputation the fifty-year-old now has.

What's actually happening

This chapter's mechanism is close cousin to Chapter 3's stalled ask, but it isn't quite the same shape, and the difference matters. The stalled ask is a single event — a raise not requested, a price increase not implemented on a specific date. The discount you keep giving yourself is chronic, ongoing, self-renewing: a price that gets re-set below its correct level again and again, at every opportunity to correct it, not because the conversation never happens but because the number chosen inside the conversation keeps landing suspiciously close to the old one.

William Samuelson and Richard Zeckhauser's 1988 research on status quo bias, introduced in Chapter 1, is the clearest lens for the specific mechanics at work. Their research demonstrated that the status quo exerts a gravitational pull independent of any conscious evaluation of whether it's actually the best option —

people default toward the current state simply because it's current, a tendency their experiments found operating even in contexts with no emotional charge attached at all, like retirement plan selections. Now add the emotional charge that a personal rate inevitably carries — a number that isn't just a business input but a felt statement about what your work, and by extension you, are worth — and the pull toward the old, familiar figure becomes considerably stronger than Samuelson and Zeckhauser's original, emotionally neutral experiments even measured. The freelancer isn't failing to do the math. She's demonstrated, three separate times, that she can do the math correctly right up until the final step, at which point something reliably pulls the outcome back toward the anchor she's most familiar with — not her current market value, but whatever number felt like "her" the longest.

The therapist's version shows the same anchor operating on someone with no old rate to defend at all, which is worth pausing on because it demonstrates the mechanism isn't strictly about defending a number you've charged before. She's never charged the higher, market-accurate rate her research supports

— there's no eleven-year history of it to feel loyal to. What she's defending instead is a number from an entirely different professional chapter of her life, one where she was a junior associate rather than a licensed, specialized practitioner building her own caseload. The anchor doesn't require prior use as a business rate to exert its pull. It only requires having once felt, at some point in your history, like an accurate reflection of your worth — even if that point was years and an entire career stage removed from the decision you're making now.

The contractor's twenty-year rate card shows what happens when status quo bias operates against overwhelming, repeated, direct external correction and still wins. Most people who underprice themselves can plausibly claim they simply don't have good market data — the freelancer's three failed attempts at least involved genuine, if abandoned, research. The contractor has something closer to two decades of unsolicited market data arriving at him directly, from competitors and clients alike, and the anchor has held anyway. This is worth sitting with, because it demonstrates that status quo bias doesn't primarily operate through a lack of information. It operates through the sheer gravitational familiarity of the current number, which can withstand an extraordinary volume of contradicting evidence as long as the evidence arrives passively rather than forcing an active decision point. The contractor absorbs the surprised reactions, the competitor comparisons, even the client questions about whether his number is a mistake — and each time, because none of those moments require him to actively choose a new number right then, the old rate card survives another year unchanged.

It's worth naming why this chapter belongs in a book about event-triggered ceilings rather than in a book about gradual drift, since on the surface a rate that never moves might sound more like creep than like a reflex. The distinction holds up under closer inspection: creep describes spending that quietly expands with no active decision behind it at all — money leaking out through a hundred small, unexamined choices. What's happening with the freelancer's rate is the opposite structure. There is an active, conscious decision point each time — the moment of actually setting the new number — and the correction happens right inside that decision point, every single time it recurs, which is precisely what makes it a repeating event-triggered reflex rather than a drift. Each pricing decision is its own separate threshold crossing, its own separate moment where the old number and the new, correctly calculated number come into direct contact, and the reflex fires fresh each time rather than accumulating passively in the background the way creep does.

How to tell the difference. Some rates genuinely shouldn't move — a market can soften, a specialty can become less scarce, a legitimate competitive pressure can cap what a service commands regardless of the provider's growing skill. The signature that distinguishes this chapter's pattern from an accurate, market-driven rate is the gap between what your own research supports and what you actually send. If you do the research honestly, arrive at a defensible number, and then watch yourself quietly revise it downward before finalizing it — with no new external information driving that revision — that specific move, the honest number followed by the unexplained discount, is the tell. A rate that stays flat because the market genuinely stayed flat requires no correction. A rate that stays flat because the research says one number and the sent invoice says a smaller one, every time, is the pattern this chapter is naming.

There's a compounding effect specific to pricing that doesn't show up as clearly in the other chapters, and it's worth naming because it explains why this particular ceiling shape is so durable: anchoring. Kahneman and Tversky's research on judgment under uncertainty, discussed elsewhere in this library, documented that initial reference points — even arbitrary ones — exert a disproportionate influence on subsequent numerical judgments, a bias that turns out to be extremely difficult to fully correct for even when a person is explicitly told the anchor is irrelevant or outdated. A rate you set years ago functions as exactly this kind of anchor for every future rate decision, regardless of how much your actual value has changed since — and because the anchor was set by you, about yourself, it carries an added layer of felt legitimacy an external, arbitrary anchor wouldn't have. It doesn't feel like an outdated data point. It feels like the truth about what you're worth, simply because it's the number you've lived inside the longest.

What it costs you

Unlike most of this book's chapters, where the cost is a discrete event — one purchase, one bet, one deal — the discount you keep giving yourself compounds silently across years, which makes it, in raw dollar terms, one of the most expensive patterns in this entire library. The freelancer's eleven years at a rate that trails her actual value by a wide and growing margin doesn't just cost the difference in any single year. It costs that difference multiplied across every year it persists, plus every future year calculated as a percentage increase off an artificially depressed base, plus the opportunity cost of the clients who would have happily paid more and never got the chance to.

The identity cost runs in an unexpected direction here, worth naming precisely because it's counterintuitive: being chronically underpriced doesn't just fail to build financial security. Over time, it can actively reinforce the very self-concept that caused it, because the chronically depressed rate becomes its own piece of confirming evidence — "I clearly can't be worth that much, look what I actually charge" — feeding directly back into the anchor for the next pricing decision. This is one of the purest feedback loops in the whole book. The old number produces a low rate. The low rate becomes new evidence for the old number. The evidence makes the next attempt to raise the rate feel even more implausible than the last one did.

There's a downstream cost worth naming too, specific to the work itself rather than just the income: chronic underpricing tends, over time, to produce chronic overwork, because the only lever left for growing revenue when the rate won't move is volume — more clients, more hours, more projects stacked on top of each other to compensate for a number that should have been higher per unit of work all along. The therapist who sets her rate forty percent below market doesn't just leave money on the table. She fills her calendar completely, turning away clients weekly, running at a capacity that would be entirely unnecessary if the rate reflected her actual value — trading her time, which is finite, for a number that a simple correction could have replaced without adding a single additional hour to her week.

The contractor's twenty years underpriced carries a cost that reaches past his own household: a business that could have supported one or two apprentices, building a genuine second generation of skilled tradespeople under his mentorship, instead operates lean enough that hiring has never felt affordable, even as the work itself has never stopped being plentiful. An accurately priced version of the same business, built on the same twenty years of skill, could plausibly have become a small local institution — training people, employing people, outliving his own retirement in some form. The rate card didn't just cap his own income. It capped the size and legacy of the entire enterprise he spent two decades building, quietly, one underpriced job at a time.

The overrides

Price from market data, not from memory. Before setting or revising any rate, gather explicit external evidence of what comparable work actually commands — three to five real data points, not a vague sense of "what feels fair." The anchor you're fighting is internal and emotional; the correction needs to be external and factual, or it will lose to the anchor every time, the way it has for eleven years running.

Set the number, then deliberately raise it once more before sending. Given how reliably this pattern shows up as a downward adjustment made at the very last step, build a counter-step into your own process: whatever number you land on through honest research, revise it upward by another ten to fifteen percent before you finalize it, specifically because you now know your default is to quietly shave the number down at the finish line. This isn't arbitrary inflation. It's a correction calibrated to a bias you've now named and can measure in your own history.

The Move: raise the rate on new clients first, and let the discomfort of the gap do the rest. Rather than trying to renegotiate every existing relationship at once, which raises the emotional stakes of every single conversation simultaneously, set your new, correctly priced rate for new clients only. Let it run for a few months. The resulting gap between what new clients pay and what long-standing ones pay becomes its own kind of pressure — uncomfortable, visible, and considerably easier to resolve by raising the old rate to match than it ever was to raise the old rate in isolation, because now you have live proof, from your own client roster, that the new number is one the market actually pays.

Ask a peer at your actual current level what they charge. Not a mentor several tiers above you, whose number will feel abstract and unreachable, and not someone earlier in their career, whose number will only reinforce the old anchor. Someone genuinely comparable, doing genuinely comparable work right now. Hearing a real, specific number from a real person at your level does something a spreadsheet of aggregate market data can't quite do on its own — it makes the correct number concrete and sayable, which matters, because the freelancer's problem was never a lack of data. It was that the data never survived contact with the moment of actually choosing a figure to send.

Track the pattern across years, not within a single decision. Keep a simple, private record of every time you've set or revised a rate, what number you landed on, and what number the actual research supported. Reviewed as a single event, one modest rate increase always looks reasonable. Reviewed across eleven years, a pattern of quietly shaving every increase down toward an old anchor becomes impossible to explain away as caution. Seeing the aggregate is often what finally makes the pattern real enough to interrupt.

Let external, repeated evidence count as data, not just as noise to be politely absorbed. For anyone in the contractor's position — evidence arriving passively, again and again, in the form of surprised clients or higher-charging competitors — the discipline is to actually log it rather than letting each instance evaporate into a vague, general sense that "people seem surprised sometimes." Every time a client comments that your price seems low, or a competitor's rate crosses your desk, write it down with a date. A handful of scattered comments is easy to dismiss. A written log spanning even six months of repeated, independent signals pointing the same direction is much harder to wave off as coincidence, and considerably harder for the old anchor to argue with.

The freelancer, once she finally sees the eleven-year pattern laid out with real dates and real numbers next to it, doesn't raise her rate all at once — the jump the math actually supports would feel, even to her, too large to send in a single email. Instead, she uses the new-client override, setting a market-accurate rate for anyone who approaches her fresh, while her existing roster stays where it's always been for one more year. Within eight months, half her client base is at the new number, not because she pushed for it, but because new clients kept saying yes to it without hesitation — proof, repeated often enough to finally be believable, that the old number had never been the ceiling of what the market would pay. It had only ever been the ceiling of what she'd let herself ask for.

The therapist, six months into her fully booked, underpriced practice, finally asks the peer question directly — messages a colleague at a comparable stage of licensure and specialization, and gets back a number nearly forty percent above her own rate sheet, stated matter-of-factly, with no hesitation on the other end at all. She raises her rate for new intakes the following week. Three people on her waitlist, offered the new number before they'd ever met her, accept without negotiating. Nobody asks why. The market had been ready for the correct number the entire time. She was the only one still living inside the old one.

The contractor, prompted by a client's offhand comment for what must be the hundredth time in twenty years, finally starts the log this chapter's override describes — a plain notebook kept in his truck, one line per instance, dated. Six months in, it holds eleven separate entries, each one independently confirming the same gap between his rate and the market's. He raises his prices eight percent, tests it on the next three bids, and loses none of them. The rate card he'd defended for two decades, it turns out, had never been protecting anything except the memory of a thirty-year-old who hadn't yet built what the fifty-year-old actually has.

That number you keep landing on isn't today's number. It's the last number that ever felt like you. Price from the evidence in front of you, not the memory underneath it.

Chapter 8 — The Raise That Didn't Last the Month

Why New Money Sometimes Disappears Faster Than Old Money Ever Did

The raise clears on a Friday, and by the following Friday, a startling amount of it is already gone — not to any single large purchase, but to a scattered, almost frantic week of smaller ones that, individually, none of which felt like much of anything at the time.

He's thirty-eight, an operations manager who has just received the largest single raise of his career, a genuine, well-earned bump after a reorganization that expanded his responsibilities considerably. He tells his wife the number that night, and they both feel, briefly, the specific lightness of a financial ceiling lifting — a feeling that, within days, curdles into something closer to itchiness. He upgrades a phone that worked fine. He books a hotel for a weekend trip he hadn't been planning. He buys a much nicer version of a jacket he was already going to buy a cheaper version of. None of these purchases, examined alone, look like anything but ordinary life.

Together, inside a single week, they add up to nearly the entire monthly value of the raise, spent before a single new paycheck reflecting it had even arrived. He isn't confused about where the money went. He genuinely could not tell you, if pressed, why that particular week felt like the right time for all of it.

This chapter's mechanism is deliberately distinguished, throughout this book, from lifestyle creep — the slow, gradual expansion of spending that happens so incrementally a person doesn't notice the drift until years later. What's happening to the operations manager is not gradual. It is event-triggered, sudden, and clustered with unusual precision around a single specific date: the date the raise was announced, not the date it started actually changing his monthly cash flow in any meaningful way. A woman running a small online retail business experiences an almost identical compression at a different scale, the week her business crosses its first month of genuine, sustainable profitability after two years of reinvesting everything back into inventory and marketing. She's built, deliberately, a plan for what that first profitable month's margin would go toward — a modest owner's draw, a cushion, the beginning of paying herself something closer to what the work is actually worth. Within days of the milestone, without really deciding to, she authorizes a significant unplanned marketing spend, justified in the moment as "striking while the momentum's there," that consumes most of the very margin the milestone represented. A month later, the business is back to breaking even, and the plan she'd built for the profit never gets to happen, not because the plan was bad, but because the profit that would have funded it disappeared inside the same week it arrived.

A high school teacher in her late twenties is informed she's being awarded a merit stipend on top of her regular salary. It's modest by the standards of the other chapters in this book, but it's the largest single bump she's received in her five years of teaching. Her situation offers a version of this pattern scaled to a much smaller number, useful precisely because the smallness makes the mechanism easier to see without the distraction of a large dollar figure. The stipend won't actually arrive for another six weeks, pending some administrative processing. In the two days after the announcement, before a single dollar has moved anywhere, she buys a new coffee maker, signs up for a subscription box she'd been considering for months, and picks up dinner out twice instead of her usual once a week — a small cluster of purchases that, added together, roughly equals the stipend she hasn't received yet. When the actual deposit lands six weeks later, she barely notices it, because psychologically, she'd already spent it the week she found out about it. The gap between the announcement and the arrival didn't slow the reflex down at all. If anything, it gave the reflex a six-week head start.

What's actually happening

The distinguishing feature of this chapter, worth stating precisely because it's the hinge the whole book turns on, is the trigger event. Lifestyle creep is a drift with no single starting point — ask someone when their spending crept up and they typically can't name a date, because there isn't one; it accumulated. What's happening here has a date, and the date is not the moment the extra money actually starts arriving in the bank account. It's the moment the news arrives — the announcement, the milestone crossed, the number seen for the first time. That timing detail matters enormously, because it tells you the trigger isn't really financial at all. It's informational.

The operations manager's actual cash flow hadn't changed at all in the week he did most of the extra spending; the raise hadn't hit a single paycheck yet. What had changed was his self-concept, the moment the new number became real to him — and the spending discharged the discomfort of that shift well before the money itself had even physically arrived.

This is self-verification theory again, but operating at a speed worth pausing on, because it clarifies something important about how fast the ceiling can fire. The dissonance between "who I believe I am, financially" and "who the new number says I now am" doesn't wait for the money to land in an account before it activates. It activates the moment the belief is updated — the moment the raise is announced, the moment the milestone is crossed and known — because the discrepancy that needs resolving is a discrepancy in self-concept, not in bank balance. The bank balance is just the eventual evidence. The identity shift is the actual trigger, and identity shifts, unlike bank transfers, happen instantly, the second new information is received. This is why the correction can outrun the money itself — spending against a raise that hasn't been paid out yet, spending against a profit margin the business technically hasn't banked yet in any accessible way. The reflex isn't responding to money in hand. It's responding to a story that just changed, and it wants that story walked back before it has time to fully settle in.

It's worth naming clearly why this chapter is the one that most often gets misdiagnosed by the people living through it, including well-meaning friends and partners who watch it happen. Because the spending is diffuse — a phone here, a hotel there, a jacket that was already on the list — it rarely registers, even to the person doing it, as a single connected event. It reads instead as "a busy week" or "a few things I'd been meaning to get anyway," each purchase evaluated on its own individual merits, none of them flagged as part of a pattern because no single one of them, viewed in isolation, looks unreasonable. This is precisely what makes this chapter's version of the ceiling so durable: the alarm purchase in Chapter 2 at least produces a single, large, nameable event a person can eventually connect to a date. This produces a dozen small, forgettable ones, scattered across a week, that resist being added up by anyone, including the person who made them, unless they go back afterward and specifically reconstruct the timeline — which almost nobody does, because nothing about any individual purchase prompts the question.

How to tell the difference. A certain amount of celebratory spending after a raise is ordinary and healthy — marking a milestone with something enjoyable is not, on its own, evidence of anything. The distinguishing feature here is proportion and completeness: does the spending in the weeks following the news roughly consume the entire value of the raise or milestone, or does it represent a modest, bounded celebration that leaves the bulk of the new money intact for its intended purpose? A single nice dinner out is proportionate. A week of scattered purchases that, added together, roughly equal a month's worth of the raise is the pattern. The test isn't whether you spent anything at all in celebration — you're allowed to. It's whether, when you add up the total honestly, the celebration turns out to have quietly consumed the entire gain.

There's a specific loss-aversion wrinkle here worth adding to the picture, distinct from the version in Chapter 3. Kahneman and Tversky's broader prospect theory work established that people evaluate outcomes relative to a reference point, and that the reference point itself is not fixed — it updates, often faster than a person consciously registers, the moment new information arrives. The instant the raise is announced, the operations manager's reference point silently moves to include it, even though the money hasn't yet appeared. Which means, from that instant forward, *not* spending against the new, not-yet-arrived money starts to feel, at a gut level, like forgoing a gain he's already come to think of as his — a subtly different and more urgent feeling than simply saving a windfall he hasn't mentally claimed yet. The itch to spend isn't recklessness. It's the reference point having moved before the actual resources caught up to it, creating a strange, compressed window where the money feels both already his and not yet real, and spending it fast is one way of resolving that specific, uncomfortable in-between state.

What it costs you

The dollar cost compounds in an unusually cruel way here, because unlike Chapter 2's alarm purchase, which at least converts money into a tangible thing — a car, an asset, something you can point to — the spending in this chapter is frequently diffuse: a scattering of small, forgettable purchases across a single week that, added up, rival the raise itself, but that don't leave behind anything the person would call an asset or even clearly remember making six months later. The operations manager's raise doesn't buy him anything he'd list if asked what he owns. It just evaporates, absorbed into a week that felt, subjectively, like nothing special.

The subtler cost is what this pattern does to the actual, felt experience of earning more. A raise that's supposed to represent forward progress — more security, more room, evidence that the effort paid off — never gets to be *felt* as any of those things, because it's gone before the person has had time to experience what having it feels like. Ask the operations manager, three months later, what changed about his life since the raise, and he'd likely struggle to answer specifically, not because the raise was small, but because it never got the chance to become anything he could point to. The forward progress was real. The experience of forward progress got quietly intercepted before it could register.

There's a compounding cost for the online retailer specifically, worth naming because it shows how this pattern can quietly stall a business's entire growth trajectory. Her plan for that first profitable month's margin wasn't self-indulgent — it was the beginning of paying herself sustainably after two years of reinvestment, the first step toward a business that could support her the way she'd built it to. When the unplanned marketing spend absorbed the margin, it didn't just cost that month's owner's draw. It reset the business to breaking even, which means the next month has to rebuild toward profitability again from scratch, and the month after that, and potentially every month after that, if the pattern repeats at every subsequent milestone. A business that keeps hitting profitability and immediately spending it away never actually becomes a profitable business in any way that compounds. It just becomes a business that touches profitability periodically and returns, each time, to where it started.

The teacher's stipend, small as it is in absolute terms, illustrates a cost worth naming precisely because the smallness makes it easy to dismiss: a pattern of spending against news before the money arrives, if it holds at this scale, will hold at every larger scale that follows — the first real promotion, the first significant bonus, eventually a inheritance or a sale of some kind, if any of those arrive later in her career. The habit doesn't recalibrate itself for larger numbers. It just repeats, proportionally, at whatever scale the next piece of good financial news happens to be. A pattern caught and corrected at the scale of a modest teaching stipend is a pattern that never gets the chance to cost her something much larger, twenty years from now, at a scale where the same six-week head start on spending would mean a considerably heavier loss.

There's a quieter relational cost worth naming in the operations manager's household specifically. He and his wife shared a genuine, warm moment the night the raise was announced — a real instance of good news landing between two people who've weathered plenty of ordinary financial stress together. That moment deserved to be the start of something, a small increment of security they could both feel accumulating. Instead, by the time she notices the credit card statement three weeks later, the warmth of that evening has curdled into something closer to a quiet, hard-to-name disappointment on her end, and a defensiveness on his — not a fight, exactly, but a small crack in the shared sense that they're building something together. The raise was supposed to be evidence of forward motion for both of them. Instead it became, without either of them quite deciding it should, a private spending spree that only one of them experienced as spending at all.

The overrides

Separate the announcement from the disbursement, deliberately, in your own head. The moment you learn about a raise, a bonus, or a profit milestone — before the money has actually changed your day-to-day cash flow — name explicitly to yourself that the news and the money are two different events. "I found out about this today. I don't actually have access to any of it yet." This sounds almost too simple, but given that the trigger in this chapter fires on the news rather than the deposit, simply delaying your own sense of "having" the money until it's genuinely accessible removes a significant part of the reflex's runway.

Automate the destination before the announcement lands, if you can see it coming. If you know a raise, bonus, or milestone is approaching, decide in advance — before the emotional charge of the actual announcement arrives — exactly where the additional money will go the moment it does. A pre-decided destination, set during a calm moment, is much harder for the reflex to override than a decision made in the emotionally compressed days right after the news, when the itch to spend is loudest.

The Move: let the first month's new money sit completely untouched, on purpose, and watch what you notice. For the first full month after any raise, bonus, or profit milestone, deliberately don't let the extra money touch your regular spending at all — route it directly into savings or debt paydown before it ever reaches an account you draw from day to day. This does two things: it removes the money from easy reach during the exact window this chapter shows is highest-risk, and it lets you observe, directly, whether the itch to spend actually fades once the money is out of view — which it very often does, because the reflex is responding to a visible, available number, not to a hidden one.

Reconstruct the timeline after the fact, at least once, so you can see what you're actually working with. If you suspect this pattern applies to you, pick your most recent raise, bonus, or milestone and go back through your spending in the four weeks that followed, purchase by purchase, with dates. Most people have never done this and are genuinely startled by what the reconstruction shows, because the pattern that was invisible in real time — a dozen small, individually defensible purchases — becomes obvious the moment it's laid out chronologically next to the date the news arrived. You don't need to do this after every windfall going forward. You need to do it once, honestly, to know whether this chapter is actually describing you.

Give the raise a name and a job before you give it a debit card. Instead of letting new money default into your general spending, assign it, specifically and in writing, to a single defined purpose the week it's announced — "this raise is my emergency fund," "this margin is my first real owner's draw." A number with an assigned job is measurably harder to spend away thoughtlessly than a number that's simply "more money now available," because spending it against its stated purpose requires a conscious override, not just a passive drift.

Treat the announcement itself as the trigger to prepare for, even when the money is still weeks away. Because this chapter's mechanism fires on news rather than on deposit, the useful discipline starts the moment you learn about a raise or stipend, not the moment it lands. The teacher's stipend was fully "spent," psychologically, within forty-eight hours of the announcement, six weeks before a dollar of it existed in her account. If you know good financial news is coming, decide what you'll do with it before you're told the exact date it arrives — the decision made in advance, before any emotional charge is attached to it, is far more durable than one made in the excited days immediately following an announcement.

The online retailer, at her next profitability milestone roughly a year later, tries something different: the moment the numbers confirm the milestone, before she tells anyone or lets herself feel the full weight of it, she moves the entire margin into a separate account labeled, simply, "owner's draw — do not touch." The urge to reinvest immediately, to "strike while the momentum's there," arrives on schedule, right around day four, exactly as it had the first time. This time, the money isn't sitting in the operating account where it's easy to redirect with a single transfer. It's somewhere with a name and a border around it, and that small structural difference turns out to be enough. The urge passes without an action attached to it, the way urges generally do when they're not immediately obeyed, and for the first time in two years of building the business, she pays herself something real.

The teacher, informed the following year of a second, larger stipend, catches herself reaching for her phone to browse subscription boxes within an hour of the email — the identical opening move as the year before, arriving with the identical speed. This time she notices the reach itself, sets the phone down, and writes one sentence on a sticky note before doing anything else: "this money isn't real yet, and I already have everything I need this week." She leaves the note on her desk for the six weeks until the deposit clears. When it finally does land, she moves it directly into the small emergency fund she's been trying to build for two years, the fund that, the previous year, the stipend had been silently spent against before it even had the chance to reach it.

The raise that vanished by the second week was never really spent on a phone, a jacket, or a hotel room — it was spent on closing the gap between the story you knew and the story that had just changed. Let the story sit unresolved for a month, and watch how much of the money is actually still there when you do.

Chapter 9 — The Room You Made Yourself Smaller In

Why Visibility Feels More Dangerous Than the Success That Earned It

The promotion announcement goes out to the whole company on a Monday morning, and by Wednesday, she's found herself apologizing for it three separate times, to three different people, none of whom asked her to.

She's forty-one, a director now, after eleven years of work that earned this without controversy — nobody on the leadership team hesitated, nobody questioned the decision, the announcement itself was warm and specific about why. And yet, in the days that follow, she catches herself doing something strange: downplaying the title in casual conversation, deflecting credit in meetings where the credit is unambiguously hers, going quieter in exactly the settings where her new role would normally call for her to speak with more authority, not less. A colleague asks, genuinely, how it feels, and she hears herself say "honestly, it's not that big a deal, the team did all the real work," which is generous but not true, and which she wouldn't have said about a much smaller accomplishment a year earlier. She isn't being modest. She's making herself smaller, on purpose, in real time, in response to a version of visibility that, days earlier, she'd have said she wanted.

A small business owner runs a related pattern after his company gets featured, unsolicited, in a well-read regional business publication — genuine, earned recognition, the kind of press most business owners spend years trying to get. In the weeks after the article runs, new customer inquiries increase noticeably, exactly as you'd expect. He responds to almost none of them promptly. He lets his website go a full month without updating the outdated pricing page the article specifically linked to. He turns down two speaking invitations that arrive directly because of the piece, each with a reasonable-sounding excuse about scheduling. None of this looks like sabotage from any single angle — everyone gets busy, everyone occasionally misses a follow-up. But the pattern, tracked across the month, shows a business owner who was moving normally before the visibility arrived and became conspicuously, uncharacteristically slow to capitalize on it the moment the visibility actually landed.

A concert violinist in her early thirties, after years of orchestra work, wins a competitive solo engagement with a well-regarded regional symphony — the kind of booking that could plausibly launch a solo career if she follows up on the relationships and momentum it generates. The performance itself goes well, genuinely well, standing ovation and glowing reviews included. In the weeks after, she's approached by two other ensembles interested in booking her, and a local arts journalist requests an interview about her path to the solo stage. She lets both booking inquiries sit unanswered long enough that one withdraws its offer, and she declines the interview outright, telling herself she doesn't have anything interesting to say yet, that she should wait until she's accomplished something more substantial before talking about her career publicly. She has, at this point, just done the most substantial thing of her career to date. The waiting isn't strategic. It's the specific, familiar discomfort of being looked at for something real, arriving right on schedule, dressed up as patience.

What's actually happening

This chapter's ceiling doesn't operate on money directly, or even on a specific deal, the way Chapter 6's did. It operates on visibility itself — the recognition, attention, and social exposure that tend to accompany financial or professional success, and that can trigger the reflex even before any additional money has actually changed hands. This matters because it shows the ceiling mechanism isn't only about dollar figures. It's about a broader felt sense of "how much space someone like me is supposed to occupy," and money is simply the most legible, most countable version of a threshold that, underneath, is really about standing, belonging, and social position.

Leon Festinger's social comparison theory, alongside Festinger's cognitive dissonance work referenced earlier in this book, is directly relevant here. Festinger's research established that people evaluate their own standing largely through comparison with others around them, and that a significant, sudden change in relative standing — even a positive one — can produce genuine discomfort, precisely because it disrupts a comparison group a person has spent years calibrated against. A promotion doesn't just change what a person does. It changes who they're now implicitly being compared to, and how they're compared to people who were, until recently, peers. That disruption is socially and psychologically costly in ways that have nothing to do with competence. The director's colleagues haven't changed how they see her — the discomfort is coming from inside her own recalibration of where she now stands relative to people she spent a decade standing beside as an equal, and making herself smaller in conversation is, at least in part, an attempt to manage that disruption before anyone else has to.

The business owner's version shows the same comparison-group disruption operating at the level of an entire community rather than a single office. His business has, for years, occupied a specific position among other local business owners — respected, established, but not the one everyone in the room is watching. The magazine feature moves him, whether he wants it or not, into a new comparison position, one where competitors and peers are now implicitly measuring themselves against him rather than the reverse. Letting the inquiries and speaking invitations sit unanswered isn't merely poor customer service. It's a way of declining to actually occupy the new position the article assigned him, quietly signaling — to himself first, and eventually to everyone watching — that the old, more comfortable comparison position is the one he still identifies with, regardless of what the article says he's become.

It's worth being precise about why this chapter closes the book rather than appearing earlier, because its placement is deliberate. Every previous chapter dealt with a number — a balance, a rate, a bet, a deal. This one deals with something that underlies all of them: the willingness to be seen occupying a higher position at all, independent of the specific dollar figure attached to it. In a real sense, this chapter's mechanism is upstream of most of the others. A person who has quietly decided, at the level of self-concept, that they're not someone who occupies significant visibility will often find ways to prevent the underlying financial success from fully arriving in the first place — declining the deal, stalling the ask, giving the windfall away — precisely because full financial success and full visibility are difficult to separate for very long. Money, past a certain point, becomes hard to hide. This is why the two people in this chapter's opening scenes weren't shrinking from a number. They were shrinking from being seen holding one.

The violinist's case sharpens this further, because unlike the director or the business owner, no money is even directly involved yet in the moments she declines — the booking inquiries and the interview request are opportunities, not deposits. What she's protecting herself from isn't a number at all. It's the beginning of a trajectory that would, if she let it run, eventually produce one: a solo career, with its own income, its own visibility, its own social comparison group entirely separate from the orchestra section she's spent a decade sitting inside as an equal among equals. Declining the interview doesn't cost her any money today. It costs her the version of her career where visibility and the number that would eventually follow it are allowed to compound together, starting now, instead of being quietly deferred to some future moment when she feels, by her own private and endlessly movable standard, sufficiently accomplished to deserve to be looked at.

There's a further mechanism specific to visibility worth adding, drawn from research on the fear of success referenced in

Chapter 6 and extended by subsequent work on what researchers have sometimes called the impostor phenomenon — first described by Pauline Clance and Suzanne Imes in 1978, in a study of high-achieving women who, despite clear external evidence of competence, persistently attributed their success to luck or error rather than ability, and lived with a chronic, private fear of being exposed as frauds. Clance and Imes's original research is specific and shouldn't be over-generalized, but the mechanism they documented — success producing not confidence but a heightened fear of exposure — maps directly onto what's happening in both scenes here. Increased visibility means increased scrutiny, and increased scrutiny, to a self-concept that hasn't yet caught up to the achievement, doesn't feel like an opportunity. It feels like an increased chance of being found out. Turning down the speaking invitation, going quiet in the meeting, letting the outdated pricing page sit unfixed — each of these, examined individually, reduces the amount of scrutiny currently pointed at the person, which is exactly what a self-concept still calibrated to a smaller, less visible version of that person would want.

How to tell the difference. Genuine humility and selective, well-considered visibility choices are not this chapter's target — plenty of accomplished people reasonably decline some opportunities because of bandwidth, fit, or simple preference, and that's healthy discernment, not a symptom. The signature to watch for is a change in baseline: did this person's rate of declining visibility, deflecting credit, or going quiet increase specifically in the weeks after a genuine promotion or recognition, relative to their own prior behavior? If someone has always been a measured, selective public presence, that's simply who they are. If someone who used to speak up, claim credit, and engage normally suddenly starts declining and deflecting right after a milestone that should, if anything, have made them more visible by default, that shift in their own baseline is the tell — not the general presence or absence of humility as a trait.

What it costs you

The dollar cost here is often indirect but substantial, because visibility, left uncapitalized, tends to be a perishable resource — the wave of attention from a press feature or a promotion announcement doesn't wait indefinitely for a person to feel ready to use it. The business owner's unanswered inquiries and declined speaking invitations don't just represent a missed month. They represent leads and relationships that, once the attention window closes, mostly don't come back around a second time. Visibility compounds when it's used and evaporates when it isn't, and this chapter's pattern specifically ensures it isn't.

The career cost is subtler and slower-moving, but arguably more significant over a long enough timeline: a pattern of shrinking at exactly the moments visibility increases tends to produce, externally, an impression of someone who's uncomfortable with growth or authority — which can, ironically, start to actually limit future opportunities for advancement, not because the person lacks the competence, but because they've trained the people around them, through repeated small acts of self-diminishment, not to expect them to want or claim the next level up. The reflex, left unexamined, doesn't just cap the current promotion's benefit. It quietly signals to everyone watching that the next one shouldn't be offered either.

There's a cost specific to the people this person leads or mentors, worth naming because visibility, unlike money, is rarely a purely private resource. A director who consistently deflects credit and minimizes her own authority isn't only shrinking her own standing — she's modeling, for everyone junior to her watching how she carries a promotion, that this is what success is supposed to look like: earned, then immediately apologized for. People learn how to inhabit success largely by watching others do it, the same social-learning mechanism referenced in this library's discussion of inherited money scripts. A leader who shrinks teaches shrinking, whether or not that's any part of her intention, simply by being the visible example everyone around her is unconsciously calibrating against.

The violinist's cost is the most quietly permanent of the three, because classical performance careers are unusually dependent on momentum that, once lost, rarely regenerates on the same terms. A solo career that could have compounded from this one well-reviewed engagement — one booking leading to another, one relationship leading to the next — instead reverts to the orchestra section she's spent a decade in, not because the door closed from the outside, but because she declined to walk through it while it was open. Doors like this one don't stay open indefinitely, and they don't reliably reopen on request. The two ensembles that reached out will very likely book someone else for their next season. The specific window in which this particular momentum could have compounded into a genuinely different career trajectory has, in all likelihood, closed — not through any external rejection, but through a delay that felt, at the time, like patience.

There's a final cost worth naming that applies to all three scenarios equally: the compounding effect of visibility avoided is genuinely different in kind from the compounding effects described in this book's other chapters. A discounted rate, an unrequested raise, a stalled deal — all of these cap a number, but the number itself remains legible, trackable, correctable once noticed, because it's still expressed in the same currency the rest of a financial life is expressed in. Declined visibility caps something less legible and, for that reason, considerably harder to notice going uncorrected: the accumulating set of relationships, referrals, and reputational momentum that would have compounded from being seen, none of which shows up on a balance sheet or a pay stub, all of which quietly determines how large the opportunities available five and ten years from now actually are. You can eventually catch an underpriced rate by comparing it to a competitor's. There's no equally clean comparison available for a career that simply grew more slowly than it could have, because nobody ever asked why.

The overrides

Notice the specific behaviors, not just the general discomfort. Deflecting credit, downplaying a title, letting a genuine accomplishment sit unmentioned when it would be natural to mention it — these are specific, nameable actions, not a vague mood. Keep a private, honest count for a few weeks after any promotion or public recognition: how many times did you specifically minimize this, in conversation or in action, when a neutral response would have been just as easy? Seeing the tally is often more persuasive than any general sense that "something feels off."

Practice occupying the new visibility in low-stakes settings first. Rather than trying to fully claim a new title or new recognition all at once, in the highest-stakes room available, practice it deliberately in smaller, safer settings — saying the new title out loud to a stranger, accepting a compliment about the achievement without immediately redirecting credit, in a conversation where little is actually riding on the outcome. This builds the same tolerance Chapter 2's override builds for a raised number, applied here to a raised social position instead.

The Move: accept one visibility opportunity you'd normally decline, specifically because it makes you uncomfortable. The next speaking invitation, press request, or public acknowledgment that arrives in the wake of a genuine accomplishment, say yes to it — not because every opportunity is worth taking on its own merits, but because saying yes specifically interrupts the pattern of automatic decline this chapter describes. Notice, afterward, that the exposure didn't produce the exposure-as-fraud catastrophe some part of you was braced for. That noticing is the actual mechanism of change, repeated enough times to outweigh the old pattern's evidence.

Separate the discomfort of visibility from an actual judgment about your readiness. The felt sense of "I'm not ready for this much attention" is not, on its own, reliable information about whether you're actually capable of handling the role, the recognition, or the opportunity — it's frequently just the sensation of a self-concept catching up to new facts, which is uncomfortable regardless of whether the new facts are accurate. Before declining a visibility opportunity, ask specifically whether you have real evidence of unreadiness, or only the felt discomfort of being newly seen. The two get confused constantly, and only one of them should actually change your decision.

Let a trusted colleague name the pattern when they see it. Ask someone who works closely with you to flag it, gently and specifically, the next time they see you deflect credit or minimize something real — not to shame you out of humility generally, humility is a fine trait in the right proportion, but to catch the specific, disproportionate version that shows up right after a genuine, earned win. An outside observer often sees the shrinking a full conversation before the person doing it does.

Respond to visibility opportunities within a fixed window, before the decline instinct has time to fully mount its case. For anyone whose pattern looks like the violinist's — genuine opportunities left unanswered until they quietly expire — set a hard rule: any inquiry connected to a real accomplishment gets a substantive response within forty-eight hours, yes or no, before the part of you that generates plausible-sounding delays has time to build its full case. Speed doesn't guarantee the right decision. It does guarantee that the decision gets made by you, deliberately, rather than by the passage of time doing the declining on your behalf.

The director, roughly six months into the new role, is invited to speak on an internal leadership panel — exactly the kind of visibility that would once have triggered an immediate, reflexive decline. She notices the old pull arrive, the urge to cite a scheduling conflict, and instead applies the override directly: she says yes, prepares seriously, and stands in front of a room of colleagues and describes, plainly and without deflection, the actual work that earned her the promotion. Nothing catastrophic follows. No one exposes her as a fraud, because there was never anything to expose. What she notices afterward, walking back to her desk, is a version of the same anticlimax the physical therapist noticed in Chapter 2 — the bracing was disproportionate to the event. The room did not, in fact, need her to be smaller in order to still like her.

The business owner, featured a second time the following year in a larger, national trade publication after his first quiet month of missed inquiries taught him something about his own pattern, sets the forty-eight-hour rule for himself before the article even runs. Every inquiry that arrives in the following weeks gets a real response within two days, yes or no. He accepts one of the two speaking invitations this time, the one that scared him more, specifically because it scared him more. The talk goes fine — better than fine, actually, generating three new client relationships he can trace directly back to that single afternoon on a stage he'd have declined a year earlier without a second thought.

That smaller version of you, the one you keep retreating into after a real win — call it what it is. Not modesty. The

ceiling, managing exposure on your behalf. Take up the space the accomplishment actually earned, and let the discomfort of being seen fade the way discomfort always does, once it's given nothing to feed on.

Before You Go

Think back to the last time you crossed a threshold that mattered — the savings goal, the raise, the deal, the milestone you'd been working toward for longer than you'd like to admit. Now think about what happened in the weeks right after. Not the celebration, if there was one. What happened to the number, specifically, in the month that followed. If you're like most people who picked up this book, something happened. Maybe it was small enough that you never connected it to the win at all. Maybe it was large enough that you've spent months since quietly confused about where the money went, telling yourself a story about bad luck or bad timing that never quite explained the whole thing. Either way, you now have a name for it, and a name changes what you're able to see the next time it happens.

You've walked through eight shapes this reflex wears. The alarm purchase, arriving days after a number you'd never seen before, spending you back down to a figure that felt survivable. The ask you kept almost making, prepared and rehearsed and abandoned at the exact threshold of the doorway. The generosity that emptied a windfall in the socially safest possible disguise, protected from scrutiny precisely because who questions kindness. The bet that didn't sound like you, reckless in a way nothing else in your financial life is reckless, arriving with suspicious precision right after a win. The deal you talked yourself out of at the finish line, sabotaged by a clause or a delay that had nothing to do with the actual terms and everything to do with who you'd have to become to close it. The discount you keep quietly giving yourself, an old number following you for years after you'd genuinely outgrown it. The raise that didn't last the month, spent not against the money itself but against the discomfort of a story that had just changed faster than your bank account had. And the room you made yourself smaller in, right when an accomplishment finally earned you more space, not less.

Here is the thesis this whole book has been building toward, worth stating plainly now that you've seen it in eight different disguises: you have an internal number for what feels like *you*, and whenever your actual life exceeds it, some part of you will act — quickly, plausibly, and quietly — to bring the evidence back in line with the belief. Not because you're self-destructive.

Not because you secretly don't want more. Because a self-concept that's been stable for decades doesn't update gracefully just because the facts changed; more often, it fights to keep the facts consistent with itself, and it's remarkably resourceful about which door it uses to do that. This book gave you eight of those doors. There are certainly more than eight. The value of learning these isn't memorizing an exhaustive list — it's training your eye to recognize the shape itself, so that whatever new door the reflex finds next, you catch the timing before the story does.

It's worth being honest, here at the close, about what this book hasn't claimed. It hasn't claimed that every large purchase, every act of generosity, every stalled negotiation, or every uncharacteristic risk is secretly this mechanism in disguise. Most of the time, a purchase is just a purchase. The evidence that matters is never a single event — it's a pattern, visible only in aggregate, only when you look back across several financial high points and notice the same reflex showing up, in different costumes, at suspiciously similar moments. One data point proves nothing. Three or four, clustered tightly around your last several thresholds, start to tell you something true about a setting you never consciously chose and have never consciously examined.

One more application worth naming before you close this book, because it comes up constantly once people start recognizing this pattern in themselves: what happens when you're sharing a financial life with someone else, and you start to suspect the ceiling belongs to them rather than to you. If you've recognized your partner in one of these chapters — the suspiciously timed purchase, the stalled negotiation they keep rescheduling, the generosity that seems to arrive right when your household finances improve — resist the urge to diagnose them from the outside, however tempting the vocabulary now feels. This book's framework is most useful as a tool for self-recognition, applied to your own patterns with your own honest access to your own internal experience. Applied to someone else, from the outside, without an invitation, it curdles quickly into something that sounds like an accusation dressed up in psychological language, which tends to produce defensiveness rather than insight. If you want to share what you've learned here with a partner whose patterns concern you, the useful move is naming your own recognition first — "I noticed this in myself, reading this book, and it made me wonder" — and letting them arrive at their own recognition, if it's there to be found, rather than handing them a diagnosis they never asked for.

If you're not yet sure whether any of this actually describes you, here is the single most useful exercise this book can leave you with, more useful than any individual chapter's overrides: take an hour, sometime this week, and build a simple timeline of your last five or six genuine financial high points — every raise, every debt payoff, every closed deal, every savings milestone, every business win you can remember over the last several years. Next to each one, write down, as honestly as you can reconstruct it, what happened financially in the four weeks that followed. Not your general sense of "things were fine" — the actual number, the actual decisions, the actual timing. Most people have never done this exercise, because each individual event felt, in the moment, complete and self-contained, disconnected from whatever came before or after it. Laid out together, with real dates, the exercise tends to produce one of two outcomes, and both are useful. Either you'll find nothing — no pattern, no suspicious clustering, just a normal financial life with its normal ups and downs — in which case you can set this book's framework aside with genuine confidence rather than lingering doubt. Or you'll find something, a repetition you hadn't consciously connected before, and now you have exactly what every chapter in this book was built to give you: not a vague feeling that something's off, but a specific, dated, visible pattern you can actually work with.

It's also worth being honest about what this book can't do on its own. No book rewires a self-concept that took decades to build in a single reading. What this book can do — what it was built to do — is make the mechanism visible enough that the next time you feel the itch right after a win, the fast reasonable-sounding purchase, the sudden generous impulse, the negotiation you're about to let slide, the finish line you're about to complicate — you have a beat of recognition available that you didn't have before. That beat is small. It is also, in practice, close to the entire difference between a ceiling that runs your finances forever and a ceiling that runs them a little less each year, as you catch it, again and again, at the exact moment it tries to fire.

Here is one practice worth carrying forward past every chapter's specific overrides, because it applies to all eight shapes at once: the next time you notice a financial decision arriving unusually fast, unusually plausible, and unusually close in time to a genuine win, pause and ask one question before you act on it — *would I be doing this if the number hadn't just changed?* You don't need a perfect answer. You need the pause itself, because the pause is the only place any of this can actually be interrupted. The reflex depends on speed. Speed is the one thing a single honest question reliably breaks.

It's worth saying plainly, here at the end, what progress against this pattern actually looks like, because it doesn't look like a straight line, and expecting one will only set you up to feel like you've failed the first time the reflex wins anyway. You will very likely catch it, cleanly, cross a threshold without a correction, and feel something like the quiet pride the physical therapist felt the second time around. You will also, some other month, miss it completely — make the alarm purchase, give away the windfall, stall the ask — and only recognize what happened weeks later, looking back with the vocabulary this book gave you. Both of those are the process working. The goal was never a permanent, one-time cure; a thermostat that took decades to calibrate doesn't recalibrate on a fixed schedule, and treating any single miss as proof that none of this worked is its own kind of all-or-nothing thinking, the same unforgiving binary the ceiling itself runs on. What actually shifts, gradually, is the ratio — more crossings held, fewer crossings corrected, the old setting losing a little authority each time you notice it and don't obey it. That ratio moving in the right direction, slowly, unevenly, over years, is what change in this specific domain actually looks like. Nobody wakes up one day with no ceiling at all. People wake up, eventually, having crossed enough thresholds cleanly that the next one stops feeling like an emergency.

There's a broader implication worth sitting with before you close this book, because it extends past any single financial decision: if the ceiling is real, then your income, your savings rate, your willingness to ask for what you're worth, are not simply functions of your skill, your market, or your effort, the way most financial advice implicitly assumes. They're also functions of an old, largely invisible setting that has been quietly capping the ceiling on all three, regardless of how good you get or how much the market would actually pay you. This is, in a strange way, good news, even though it doesn't always feel like it while you're catching yourself mid-reflex. Skill takes years to build. Markets are largely outside your control. A setting, once it's been found and named, can move considerably faster than either of those — not overnight, but faster, because it was never actually about your competence in the first place. It was about a number a much younger version of you decided on, with incomplete information, a long time ago. That number was always negotiable. It just never had anyone push back on it before.

If you take nothing else from these pages, take this: the ceiling was installed by a version of you working with old information, trying to keep you safe inside circumstances that, in all likelihood, no longer describe your life at all. It did its job once. It doesn't know the job is finished. Every time you cross a threshold and don't let the reflex quietly walk you back down from it — every time you sit with the discomfort instead of discharging it, ask instead of stalling, give a considered amount instead of an erasing one, apply your normal diligence instead of skipping it, send the email instead of adding the clause, price from the evidence instead of the memory, let the raise sit instead of spending the story, take up the space instead of shrinking from it — you're not just keeping one number where it belongs. You're teaching an old thermostat, one crossing at a time, that the room can run warmer now, and nothing is going to catch fire because of it.

One last practical note, because it matters and shouldn't go unsaid: nothing in this book replaces a real conversation with a financial advisor, a business mentor, or a trusted professional if what you're facing involves genuinely complex decisions — structuring a windfall, planning around a major liquidity event, negotiating equity, building a pricing strategy for a growing business. This book's job was narrower and came first: clearing the internal reflex out of the way so that when you do sit down with that advisor, that mentor, that professional, you're making the decision with a clear head instead of an old thermostat quietly voting against your own progress. Get the reflex out of the way. Then get the strategy from people whose job is the strategy, not the psychology underneath it.

Think, one last time, about the people who walked through these pages with you — not because their specific stories matter more than yours, but because their range says something worth carrying forward. A physical therapist and a schoolteacher and a retired schoolteacher who'd never met each other, an architect and a landscaper who work in different trades entirely, a violinist and a veterinarian who have nothing professionally in common, a freelance designer and a tech founder separated by a hundred times the money — all of them, at some financial or professional high point in their very different lives, ran a version of the identical reflex. That range is the point. This mechanism doesn't care about your industry, your income bracket, your level of education, or how impressive your resume looks from the outside. It cares only about the gap between what you have and what an old, unexamined number once decided you were allowed to have. Close enough attention to that gap, in your own life, at your own next threshold, is the only thing any of these people actually needed to start closing it.

And notice, too, what happened to nearly every one of them once they caught the pattern even once. The physical therapist crossed a second, higher threshold and simply stayed there. The illustrator, at her next opportunity, set a hard deadline for herself instead of a slow drift of clarifying questions. The freelancer built a new-client pricing floor that eventually pulled her whole roster upward. None of them became different people. None of them woke up one morning suddenly free of the old wiring. What changed, each time, was smaller and more specific than that: one threshold, crossed cleanly, where a threshold had previously been crossed and then quietly walked back. That's not a transformation story. It's a single data point, repeated enough times to become a new habit sitting on top of an old reflex that never fully disappears but slowly loses its authority to run the show uncontested. That's what change actually looks like here, and it's more available to you, starting at your very next threshold, than four decades of an unexamined setting might currently have you believe.

You didn't build the thermostat. A younger version of you did, with the only information available at the time, trying to keep you safe. That version did their job. You get to finish it — not by never feeling the pull again, but by feeling it, naming it, and crossing the threshold anyway, until the number that once felt like an alarm starts, slowly, to feel like nothing more than the truth about where you actually are.

Notes & Further Reading

The psychological research referenced throughout this book is real, attributable, and, where possible, traceable to primary sources. This section is offered so you can go deeper into any mechanism that particularly resonated, rather than taking this book's summary as the final word on any of it.

Self-verification theory — William B. Swann Jr.'s foundational work on self-verification, including *"Self-Verification Theory,"* has been developed across numerous papers and summarized in accessible form in Swann's contributions to social psychology handbooks. His research on people seeking confirmation of existing self-views, including unflattering ones, is among the most replicated findings in the self-concept literature and underlies the framework this book calls "the ceiling."

Self-discrepancy theory — E. Tory Higgins's self-discrepancy theory was introduced in his 1987 paper "Self-Discrepancy: A Theory Relating Self and Affect," published in *Psychological Review*. Higgins's distinction between the actual, ideal, and ought selves, and the different emotional signatures produced by discrepancies between them, is foundational to the framework used throughout this book, especially Chapter 1 and Chapter 3.

Status quo bias — William Samuelson and Richard Zeckhauser's paper "Status Quo Bias in Decision Making," published in the *Journal of Risk and Uncertainty* in 1988, documented the systematic preference for current states of affairs independent of their objective merit, including in emotionally neutral contexts. This book applies their framework to pricing and personal financial thresholds in Chapters 1 and 7.

Prospect theory and loss aversion — Daniel Kahneman and Amos Tversky's "Prospect Theory: An Analysis of Decision under Risk," published in *Econometrica* in 1979, is the foundational text for the loss-aversion and reference-point concepts used throughout this book, particularly in Chapters 3, 5, and 8. Kahneman's later book *Thinking, Fast and Slow* (2011) offers an accessible synthesis of this and related work for general readers. The "house money effect" extending prospect theory into gambling and windfall contexts draws on subsequent research by Richard Thaler and Eric Johnson, among others, in the behavioral finance literature.

Cognitive dissonance — Leon Festinger's *A Theory of Cognitive Dissonance* (1957) remains the foundational text on the discomfort produced by conflicting cognitions and the behavioral routes people take to resolve it, referenced in Chapter 4. Festinger's separate and equally foundational work, "A Theory of Social Comparison Processes," published in *Human Relations* in 1954, underlies the discussion of visibility and relative standing in Chapter 9.

Moral licensing — The concept of moral licensing, including the specific mechanism by which virtuous acts can license subsequent behavior, has been studied by researchers including Nina Mazar and Chen-Bo Zhong, notably in their 2010 paper "Do Green Products Make Us Better People?" published in *Psychological Science*, which examines the broader phenomenon this book applies to generosity in Chapter 4.

Money scripts and early financial socialization — The framework of money scripts, describing the largely unconscious beliefs about money absorbed in early childhood, was developed by Brad Klontz, Ted Klontz, and later Sonya Britt, notably in their 2011 paper "Money Beliefs and Financial Behaviors: Development of the Klontz Money Script Inventory," published in the *Journal of Financial Therapy*. This body of work underlies the discussion in Chapter 1 of where the ceiling's original setting tends to be installed, and is referenced elsewhere in this library's discussion of inherited family money patterns.

Social learning theory — Albert Bandura's broader work on social learning, distinct from but related to his self-efficacy research cited above, is documented across his career and most notably in his 1977 book *Social Learning Theory*. It underlies the discussion in Chapter 1 and Chapter 9 of how children absorb emotional patterns around money through observation rather than direct instruction, and how leaders model financial and visibility behavior for those who work under them.

Self-efficacy — Albert Bandura's extensive body of work on self-efficacy, most comprehensively presented in his 1997 book *Self-Efficacy: The Exercise of Control*, establishes the framework used in Chapter 6 regarding how belief in one's own capacity shapes behavior, often in self-fulfilling ways.

Fear of success — Matina Horner's early research on fear of success was published in her 1968 doctoral dissertation and subsequent papers in the late 1960s and early 1970s. The concept has been refined and contextualized by later researchers, and this book references it as one contributing lens among several in Chapter 6 and Chapter 9, not as a complete or uncontested account.

Self-handicapping — Edward E. Jones and Steven Berglas's foundational paper "Control of Attributions About the Self Through Self-Handicapping Strategies," published in *Personality and Social Psychology Bulletin* in 1978, established the framework for understanding how people sometimes create obstacles to their own success, referenced in Chapter 5.

Impostor phenomenon — Pauline Rose Clance and Suzanne Imes's original 1978 paper, "The Impostor Phenomenon in High Achieving Women: Dynamics and Therapeutic Intervention," published in *Psychotherapy: Theory, Research & Practice*, is the source of the concept referenced in

Chapter 9. Later research has expanded the concept beyond Clance and Imes's original population, and this book treats it as one contributing mechanism among several rather than a universal explanation.

Approach-avoidance conflict — The foundational framework for approach-avoidance conflict originates in Kurt Lewin's field theory work from the 1930s and was substantially developed by later researchers including Neal Miller, whose experimental work through the mid-twentieth century established the behavioral dynamics referenced in Chapter 3.

Anchoring — Amos Tversky and Daniel Kahneman's "Judgment under Uncertainty: Heuristics and Biases," published in *Science* in 1974, is the foundational source for the anchoring effect referenced in Chapter 7, alongside their broader prospect theory work cited above.

This book has aimed, throughout, to represent each of these bodies of research accurately and to avoid overstating what any single study or theory can claim. Where a mechanism is presented as one contributing lens rather than a complete explanation, that framing is intentional — human financial behavior is rarely the product of a single, clean psychological cause, and this book has tried to resist the temptation to claim otherwise for the sake of a tidier chapter.

A note on how this book uses research, since it's worth being transparent about the method rather than letting citations imply more certainty than the underlying science supports. None of the studies referenced above were conducted specifically on "ceiling" behavior as this book defines it — that specific framing, and the eight-chapter structure built around it, is this book's own synthesis, offered as a genuinely useful lens rather than as an established clinical diagnosis with a formal name in the literature. What is well-established, and what this book has been careful to draw only from established findings for, are the underlying component mechanisms: that people are motivated to verify existing self-concepts even at a cost (Swann), that discrepancies between actual and internalized standards produce specific emotional signatures (Higgins), that people default toward familiar states independent of merit (Samuelson and Zeckhauser), that gains and losses are weighted asymmetrically relative to a reference point (Kahneman and Tversky), and so on through each mechanism cited above. This book's contribution is connecting those well-documented pieces into a coherent account of a pattern many readers will recognize from their own lives — a synthesis, not a new discovery, and one you're encouraged to hold with the same appropriate skepticism you'd bring to any framework that claims to explain something as complicated as another person's relationship with money, including your own.

It's also worth noting explicitly what this book does not claim clinical or diagnostic authority over. If patterns described in this book are accompanied by broader symptoms of anxiety, depression, or compulsive behavior that significantly interfere with daily functioning, that's a conversation for a licensed mental health professional, not a self-help book. The mechanisms described here are common, ordinary features of how self-concept interacts with money for a very large number of otherwise well-functioning people — not, in themselves, evidence of a clinical condition. Most of what this book describes is closer to a widespread, under-named habit of mind than to a disorder, and it's treated that way throughout: as something to notice and gradually adjust, not something to be alarmed about.

A final note on the case studies used throughout this book. The physical therapist, the software developer, the schoolteacher, the woman preparing to ask for a raise, the restaurant owner, the illustrator, the designer closing a large contract, the tech founder, the nurse practitioner, the consultant with the cryptocurrency position, the retail worker paying off debt, the veterinarian made partner, the architect and his stalled email, the therapist offered a partnership, the landscaper underbidding a contract, the freelancer who's raised her rate twice in eleven years, the therapist building a solo caseload, the contractor with the twenty-year-old rate card, the operations manager and his raise, the online retailer's profitability milestone, the teacher's merit stipend, the newly promoted director, the small business owner featured in a magazine, and the concert violinist — every one of these is a composite, constructed to illustrate a real and well-documented psychological mechanism rather than a report of any specific individual's life. None of them is a disguised account of a real client, patient, or acquaintance. The scenarios are built to be representative and recognizable, not biographical, and any resemblance to a specific real person's circumstances is coincidental. What is not fictional is the underlying psychology each scenario is built to illustrate — that part is drawn directly from the cited research, and held, throughout, to the standard of being real, attributable, and accurately represented.

About This Book

The Ceiling Instinct is part of The Money Instinct library, a series exploring the specific, nameable psychological patterns that quietly shape how people earn, hold, spend, and relate to money — not through generic advice, but through close, honest attention to the mechanisms actually running underneath everyday financial behavior. Where other volumes in this library examine how people hide from their own numbers, how they underearn relative to their actual value, and how inherited shame distorts an otherwise ordinary relationship with money, this volume turns to a narrower and more specific question: what happens in the exact moment success itself arrives, and why does arrival so often trigger retreat.

This book does not offer investment advice, tax guidance, or specific financial recommendations, and nothing in it should be treated as a substitute for consultation with a qualified financial, legal, or tax professional. Its aim is narrower and, hopefully, more durable: to help you recognize a pattern clearly enough that you can catch it the next time it fires, in your own life, in real time — which is the only place any of this can actually be changed.

If this book helped you see something in yourself you hadn't been able to name before, the most useful next step isn't necessarily another book. It's the next threshold you're approaching right now, today, this month — the raise you haven't asked for, the price you haven't corrected, the deal that's close to closing, the milestone you can already feel coming. Watch what happens in the weeks after you cross it. That's the whole practice. Not a system, not a program — just watching, closely, with a name now available for what you're watching for.

This book was written for a specific reader, and it may help to say plainly who that reader is, so you can gauge whether the fit was right. It's written for someone whose income or net worth has grown, or is poised to grow, faster than their sense of self has had time to catch up with — the person who keeps having good financial news happen to them and keeps finding a way to make it not quite stick. It is not written for someone in acute financial hardship looking for tactical debt or budgeting advice, and it isn't written as a guide to building wealth from nothing; other books, including others in this library, serve those readers better. This book assumes you are already, in some real sense, succeeding — and its entire concern is the specific, quiet way that success keeps getting undone by the very person who earned it.

It's also worth naming, honestly, who this book is not for, or at least not primarily for: someone whose financial setbacks are being driven mainly by external circumstances — a genuinely difficult job market, a health crisis, a structurally unequal system stacked against them — will not find this book's framework especially useful, because the mechanism described here is specifically about self-generated corrections following self-generated success, not about the very real external headwinds many people face that have nothing to do with an internal ceiling. Applying this book's lens to a situation that's actually about external constraint would be a category error, and a subtly unkind one — this book has tried, throughout, to be precise about which problem it's actually solving, and this is the boundary of that precision.

If you found value in this volume, the rest of The Money Instinct library explores other shapes this same territory takes — the instinct to hide your numbers from the people closest to you, the instinct to earn less than you're worth, the instinct to carry shame that was never yours to carry, and others, each one a different angle on the same underlying question: not how to make more money, but how to stop being the reason it doesn't stay.

A closing word on how to actually use this book, since a book like this can be read in very different ways with very different results. Reading it once, cover to cover, will give you the vocabulary — the eight shapes, the underlying mechanism, the sense of recognition that comes from finally having language for a pattern you'd only ever felt before. That's valuable, and it's probably why you picked this book up. But the vocabulary alone won't do the actual work. The actual work happens later, at your next real threshold — the next raise, the next milestone, the next deal that's close to closing — when the old pull arrives and you have, for the first time, a choice about whether to follow it. Consider keeping this book somewhere you'll actually see it again: not filed away once finished, but close at hand, so that when you feel the specific itch this book describes, you can turn back to the relevant chapter in the moment that actually matters, rather than trying to remember, days later, what you were supposed to do differently. A book about a reflex is only useful if it's available at the speed the reflex operates.

A note on rereading, since this is the kind of book that tends to land differently on a second pass. The first read gives you recognition — the shock of seeing your own life described accurately by a stranger. A second read, taken later, after you've actually lived through a threshold or two with this book's vocabulary in hand, tends to give you something more useful: precision. You'll likely find, on a second pass, that one or two chapters that felt only mildly relevant the first time now read as exactly, specifically your pattern, because you'll have real, lived evidence by then to test the framework against, rather than just the recognition of a familiar feeling. Books about reflexes are rarely fully absorbed in one sitting, because the reflex itself has to actually fire, at least once, with the book's language available, before the language becomes truly your own rather than borrowed.

Also in the Series

Every book in The Money Instinct library stands on its own — read them in any order. If this one was useful, the library continues:

The Money Instinct

The Secrecy Instinct

The Underearning Instinct

The Shame Instinct

The Panic Instinct

The Merge Instinct

The Windfall Instinct

The Control Instinct

The Legacy Instinct

The Comparison Instinct

The Enabling Instinct

The Austerity Instinct

The Paralysis Instinct

The Retirement Instinct

The Divorce Instinct

The Enough Instinct

The Overconfidence Instinct

The Vigilance Instinct

The Generosity Instinct

www.ingramcontent.com/pod-product-compliance
Lightning Source LLC
LaVergne TN
LVHW030725061126
851857LV00019B/2000
* 9 7 8 1 8 0 4 2 8 1 0 3 1 *